SECONDARY RESEARCH

Applied Social Research Methods Series
Volume 4

Applied Social Research Methods Series

Series Editor:
LEONARD BICKMAN, Peabody College, Vanderbilt University

Series Associate Editor:
DEBRA ROG, Joint Legislative Audit and
Review Commission, Commonwealth of Virginia

This series is designed to provide students and practicing professionals in the social sciences with relatively inexpensive softcover textbooks describing the major methods used in applied social research. Each text introduces the reader to the state of the art of that particular method and follows step-by-step procedures in its explanation. Each author describes the theory underlying the method to help the student understand the reasons for undertaking certain tasks. Current research is used to support the author's approach. Examples of utilization in a variety of applied fields, as well as sample exercises, are included in the books to aid in classroom use.

Volumes in this series:

1. **SURVEY RESEARCH METHODS**, Floyd J. Fowler, Jr.

2. **THE INTEGRATIVE RESEARCH REVIEW: A Systematic Approach**, Harris M. Cooper

3. **METHODS FOR POLICY RESEARCH**, Ann Majchrzak

4. **SECONDARY RESEARCH: Information Sources and Methods**, David W. Stewart

5. **CASE STUDY RESEARCH: Design and Methods**, Robert K. Yin

6. **META-ANALYTIC PROCEDURES FOR SOCIAL RESEARCH**, Robert Rosenthal

Additional volumes currently in development

SECONDARY RESEARCH

Information Sources and Methods

David W. Stewart

Applied Social Research Methods Series
Volume 4

 SAGE PUBLICATIONS Beverly Hills London New Delhi

For information address:

SAGE Publications, Inc.
275 South Beverly Drive
Beverly Hills, California 90212

SAGE Publications India Pvt. Ltd.
C-236 Defence Colony
New Delhi 110 024, India

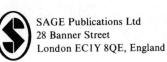
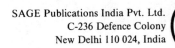

SAGE Publications Ltd
28 Banner Street
London EC1Y 8QE, England

Printed in the United States of America

Library of Congress Cataloging in Publication Data

Stewart, David W.
    Secondary research.

    (Applied social research methods texts ; 4)
    Bibliography: p.
    1. Social sciences—Research. I. Title. II. Series.
H62.S7547   1984   300′.72   84-9879
ISBN 0-8039-2338-4
ISBN 0-8039-2339-2 (pbk.)

SECOND PRINTING, 1985

SECONDARY RESEARCH

CONTENTS

PREFACE

Many researchers and students have a general fear of libraries and the stacks of printed matter within them. Few know of the wealth of information available on a wide range of topics. Businesses and government organizations often spend considerable sums of money to obtain information that is then freely available to the rest of us. This monograph is designed as an introduction to locating, using, evaluating, and integrating this information. The emphasis is on material that is most useful for more common applications. It is not intended as a compendium of all available source materials, but it will take the reader quite far into a literature search.

Finding information is but the first step in using secondary sources. Once sources have been identified, the information must be obtained, evaluated, and integrated. Inconsistencies within and among sources must be resolved. Data may have to be creatively combined to find the answer to a specific question. Chapter 2 provides a discussion of issues in evaluating research, while Chapter 8 deals with the problem of integrating data and information from multiple sources.

Chapters 3, 4, 5, and a portion of Chapter 1 introduce information sources. These are primarily printed media, but may also include experts, trade associations, and other sources of information. Chapter 6 introduces the growing capability for computer-assisted information searches. Chapter 7 provides two brief examples of literature searches to demonstrate how to use the various sources of information introduced in earlier chapters.

This book was designed as a reference book and supplement to more traditional social science research texts. It grew out of my own teaching of courses on marketing research and planning, and my need for a good supplement to traditional texts, a supplement that would provide a readable guide to secondary sources. Due to the sheer volume of secondary source material, the vast majority of the information available is not covered, even in this work. My own experience with secondary sources and with attempting to teach students to use secondary information suggests that there is no substitute for some practical hands-on experience. The exercises provided at the ends of the chapters are designed to provide that experience. However, other exercises, perhaps more relevant to a given course of discipline, should not be difficult to devise. Like any other type of research, secondary research is best learned by doing.

As with any project, this book is the product of not only my labor but also that of others. A special word of appreciation is due Gretchen Diemer and Maureen Writesman, who typed the manuscript, and Connie Pechmann, who proofread and edited the manuscript. Obviously, any remaining errors are my responsibility. Thanks also to my wife Lenora and my daughter Sarah, who tolerated late-night work and a preoccupied husband/ father. Finally, I dedicate the book to Rachel Dawn, who came into the world as I completed the manuscript.

— David W. Stewart
Nashville, Tennessee

1

Introduction

Secondary information consists of sources of data and other information collected by others and archived in some form. These sources include government reports, industry studies, and syndicated information services as well as the traditional books and journals found in libraries. Secondary information offers relatively quick and inexpensive answers to many questions and is almost always the point of departure for primary research.

A mainstay of virtually every research effort is the use of published statistical material and information not specifically gathered for the research question at hand. Such information is called *secondary data*. These data were collected for some general information need or as a part of a research effort designed to answer a specific question. Secondary data come in many forms, ranging from large statistical studies published by the federal government and other government bodies to the unpublished observations of a knowledgeable observer. A vast international information industry has come into being since the 1950s. This industry obtains, stores, and even sells information in one form or another. The computer has added great power to the capacity of individuals and organizations to identify and use this information.

The raw data collected by others may be generally available to the general public, but more likely these data are summarized and reported in summary form. Such published summaries are often referred to as *secondary sources*. The term *secondary information* is frequently used to refer to both secondary data (the raw data obtained in various studies) and secondary sources (the published summaries of these data). In the remainder of this book, these terms will be used interchangeably, because the distinctions among these types of information tend to blur in practice. The use of secondary information is often referred to as *secondary analysis* (or research). Secondary analysis is simply a further analysis of information that has already been obtained. Such an analysis may be related to the original purpose for which the data were collected, or may address an issue quite different from that which prompted the original data gathering effort. It may involve the integration of information from several sources or a reanalysis of the data of a single source.

Most research efforts begin with some type of secondary analysis. An investigation of secondary sources provides an opportunity to learn what is already known, and what remains to be learned, about a particular topic. It may suggest methods for studying a particular problem. It is often possible to combine the information from several different sources to reach conclusions that are not suggested by any one source. Indeed, theory building in the social sciences frequently takes the form of integrating the findings of multiple empiricial studies within a single general framework.

Secondary research differs from *primary research* in that the collection of the information is not the responsibility of the analyst. In secondary research, the analyst enters the picture after the data collection effort is over. In primary research, the analyst is responsible for the design of the research, the collection of the data, and the analysis and summary of the information. In some situations, primary and secondary research are substitutes. For example, if one were interested in the transportation habits of individuals in a large metropolitan area, a survey of a representative sample of the residents of the area would be appropriate. Such a survey would involve primary research. The analyst might design a questionnaire requesting information about the use of various modes of transportation, types of trips taken during some time interval, preference for various means of transportation, and other relevant information. The survey instrument (questionnaire) could be mailed to a sample of residents of the metropolitan area. As the questionnaires were returned, the analyst would tabulate responses and summarize the data.

An alternative method for investigating the same issue could involve secondary research. If a study of the transportation habits of the metropolitan area had been conducted recently by someone else, it might be possible to answer all of the questions about transportation habits by referring to that study. In fact, the U.S. Bureau of the Census carries out a census of transportation that includes a survey of transportation habits. Rather than conducting his or her own study, the analyst may use the data collected by the Census Bureau. Use of Census Bureau data has the advantages of being less expensive and providing answers more quickly than primary research. The disadvantage of using this secondary source is that questions of interest may not be addressed in the Census Bureau survey or may have been asked in a fashion that is not consistent with the analyst's current interests.

More often, primary and secondary research are used in a complementary fashion, rather than as substitutes for one another. Research efforts generally begin with a question or set of objectives. These objectives are met and the question answered through the acquisition of information. The source of this information — whether it is obtained by secondary or primary research — is really not important as long as the information is trustworthy and answers the question at hand. In fact, it will be less expensive and time-consuming to use secondary sources. Frequently, however, at least some of the questions at hand have not been answered by prior research; this requires primary research. In these cases, secondary research helps define the agenda for subsequent primary research by suggesting which questions require answers that have not been obtained in previous research. Secondary data may also identify the means by which the primary research should be carried out: (1) questions that should be addressed, (2) measurement instruments such as questionnaires, and (3) relevant respondents.

In applied settings, such as government agencies, corporations, and other organizations, information is required for administrative decisions. Since there is generally some cost to obtaining information by primary research, it is more efficient to use secondary research when it is available. Identifying what is already known and available in secondary sources also ensures that funds are expended only for the acquisition of new information. A thorough knowledge of secondary information tends to enhance the efficiency of primary research efforts.

Curiously, many individuals and organizations do not take full advantage of the array of secondary information available to them. This is in part the result of the information explosion that has occurred in the last twenty years and the lack of a systematic guide to secondary sources. Yet it is hard to conceive of a research effort that does not begin with at least some secondary research. Existing information provides a foundation for problem formulation, for the design of new research, and for the analysis and interpretation of new information. There is little point in rediscovering that which is already known. The purpose of primary research should generally be to fill in gaps in existing knowledge. These gaps cannot be identified without an understanding of the existing knowledge base. It is, perhaps, unfortunate that the term "secondary" has been chosen to refer to existing data. This term does not imply anything about the importance of the information, only that it is being used for research beyond the specific informational need that prompted the original gathering of the data. All primary research may ultimately become someone else's secondary source. In the remainder of this book, secondary sources will be examined. Specific sources and how they might be used will be addressed, but first the advantages and disadvantages of secondary information will be discussed.

ADVANTAGES OF SECONDARY INFORMATION

Secondary information has some distinctive advantages over primary data collection efforts. The more significant of these advantages are related to time and cost. In general, it is much less expensive to use secondary data than it is to conduct a primary research investigation. This is true even where there are costs associated with obtaining the secondary data. When answers to questions are required quickly, the only practical alternative is to consult secondary sources. If stringent budget and time constraints are imposed on primary research, secondary research may provide higher-quality data than could be obtained with a new research project.

Secondary sources provide a useful starting point for additional research by suggesting problem formulations, research hypotheses, and research methods. Consultation of secondary sources provides a means for increasing the efficiency of the research dollar by targeting real gaps and oversights in knowledge. Secondary data also provide a useful comparative tool. New data may be compared to existing data for purposes of examining differences or trends. It may also provide a basis for determining whether or not new information is representative of a population, as in the case of sampling. Comparison of the demographic characteristics of a sample to those of the larger population, as specified by the Bureau of the Census, may reveal how representative the sample is of the larger population.

DISADVANTAGES OF SECONDARY INFORMATION

Secondary sources are not without problems. As in primary research, the design or conclusions may be flawed. Data are often collected with a specific purpose in mind, a purpose that may produce deliberate or unintentional bias. Thus secondary sources must be evaluated carefully. Chapter 2 is devoted to the evaluation of secondary information. The fact that secondary data were collected originally for particular purposes may produce other problems. Category definitions, particular measures, or treatment effects may not be the most appropriate for the purpose at hand. Seldom are secondary data available at the individual-observation level. This means that the data are aggregated in some form, and the unit of aggregation may be inappropriate for a particular purpose. Finally, secondary data are, by definition, old data. Thus the data may not be particularly timely for some purposes.

SOURCES OF SECONDARY DATA

Secondary data are available from a variety of sources and in a variety of forms, although the single largest and most frequently consulted source is a library. Libraries differ in the kinds of materials they have available. University libraries tend to carry academically relevant materials. Public libraries carry more general interest and business-relevant materials. Government libraries handle government documents, and commercial libraries carry documents of interest to clients. Many commercial organizations, corporations, and research firms also maintain their own specialized libraries, which they may allow others to use. The single best guide to a library is its reference librarian. This individual is a specialist with training in information sources who can often provide guidance to the most relevant information for a particular purpose. Many organizations have information officers or librarians whose function it is to assist others in locating information. Public and commercial libraries have developed information hotlines for their patrons' specific questions. Many libraries are responsive to their users' needs for various information resources and welcome suggestions.

University and public libraries do not carry academic literature only. There is a substantial amount of information produced by government agencies, corporations, trade and professional associations, and other organizations that many libraries will carry. These sources can be quite general, as in the case of government census data, or quite specific, as in the case of trade journals such as *Beverage World* or *Progressive Grocer*. The magnitude of available information necessitates access to general guides and indices to this literature. These guides represent an important access point to secondary literature. Table 1.1 provides a listing of some of the more common guides and directories to general secondary sources. Guides to more academic literature sources are described in Table 1.2. The sources listed in these two tables represent good starting points for a library search, but libraries are not the only sources of secondary information — there are many others including the following:

(1) *Experts and authorities:* A good starting point for learning about a topic is someone who is well acquainted with the topic, perhaps someone who has been involved in research on the topic. For example, one researcher, after an exhaustive search of the biological and veterinary medicine literature, finally obtained the information he needed by telephoning veterinary schools until he located an authority on the topic. The information required was simple (how much food does an adult cat consume in a day), but was essential for estimating the market potential for a new pet food.

Trade and professional associations, chambers of commerce, executives, and researchers are all important sources of information. Much valuable information consists of information obtained through experience. Sorted impressions and conclusions based on experience are often the only sources of information on some topics. A few telephone calls to knowledgeable experts are sometimes all that is required to obtain a piece of information, and there are situations in which such expert opinion is the *only* source of information. Clearly, however, such information must be carefully evaluated and opinion separated from fact. This is not always easily accomplished, particularly in the case of value-laden topics. A good question to ask such experts is how they know something to be the case.

(2) *Recorded data and records:* Nearly every organization generates data as a normal part of its operations. Letters, memoranda, sales contracts, purchase orders, accounting records, personnel records, and so on are all potentially valuable sources of information. Such information is not always accessible, but often it is. Usually such information must be reorganized and reanalyzed in a different form, however. This is particularly true of routine operating information from organizations.

(3) *Commercial information services:* Numerous firms are in the business of collecting and selling information. Such information is unlikely to be available in libraries as long as it has commercial value. A variety of the information services offered by these firms will be reviewed in subsequent chapters. Although such information is costly, it is often less expensive and more practical to use than information obtained by doing a comparable study of one's own.

Many researchers approach the secondary research activity with trepidation. Until one has become familiar with them, libraries can be imposing operations, and there may be a sense of embarrassment associated with approaching experts in a field. Once one is acquainted with how to access information, however, libraries become vital resources.

Secondary sources are a vital resource for all social scientists, but may be more important for the applied researcher than for the researcher engaged in more basic research. Basic research is primarily concerned with producing new knowledge and with filling gaps that exist in current knowledge. Secondary data thus serve as starting points for the basic researcher. These are points of departure that the basic researcher seeks to go beyond. The applied researcher, on the other hand, is more often concerned with using knowledge that already exists, at least in some form, for the solution of a specific problem. For the applied researcher, primary research is required only when secondary information does not provide answers to specific questions. Thus, for the social scientist working in an

(text continues on page 22)

TABLE 1.1
General Directories and Guides to Secondary Source Material

Applied Science and Technology Index

A subject index to over 200 journals in aeronautics, space science, energy, engineering, fire and fire prevention, chemistry, computer technology, food and food industries, geology, machinery, mathematics, mineralogy, metallurgy, oceanography, petroleum and gas, physics, plastics, textiles and fabrics, and transportation.

AUBER Bibliography

An annual compilation of books, monographs, working papers, articles, and other publications related to business and economics.

Business Index

An index providing subject coverage of 325 business periodicals and newspapers as well as business information from some 1100 general and legal periodicals. Published monthly since 1979.

Business Information Sources

A bibliography of references in business and economics.

Business Periodicals Index

A subject index to 150 periodicals in the field of business. Published since 1959.

The Directory of Directories

An annual compilation of directories. This is a guide to guides, indexed by subject matter and title.

Marketing Information Guide

An annotated bibliography of recently published books, government documents, periodical articles, and other materials on a wide range of topics related to marketing. Published by U.S. Department of Commerce.

Monthly Catalog of U.S. Government Publications

A listing of the publications of the U.S. government.

Public Affairs Information Service Bulletin

A biweekly subject index to books, pamphlets, government documents, periodical articles, and other publications related to socioeconomic conditions and public affairs.

New York Times Index

A guide to the contents of the *New York Times*; includes brief summaries of articles.

Reader's Guide to Periodical Literature

A directory containing subject and author indexes of more than 150 general publications in the United States. Published semimonthly since 1900.

(continued)

TABLE 1.1 Continued

Trade and Industry Index

An index providing complete listing and selective abstracts of 275 trade and industry journals and selective indexing of 1200 additional publications.

Wall Street Journal Index

A guide to the contents of the *Wall Street Journal*. Two separate sections are published: one for general news and the other for corporate news.

NOTE: Complete bibliographic information for each of these publications and all others mentioned in this book appears in the References section.

TABLE 1.2
Guides to Academic Literature

Abstracts of Hospital Management Studies

A guide to articles, books, and monographs related to hospital and health care management.

America: History and Life

An index published in three parts: (A) Article Abstracts and Citations, (B) Index to Book Reviews, and (C) American History Bibliography. Indexes articles on ethnic studies, folklore, history, politics and government, urban affairs, and related topics.

Communication Abstracts

A quarterly index of major articles, books, and monographs related to communication. Abstracts of indexed publications are included.

Current Index to Journals in Education

An index to articles in approximately 700 journals in education and related fields. Published by the Educational Resources Information Center (ERIC).

Dissertation Abstracts International

A publication including titles, key words, and author indices for doctoral dissertations in over 350 institutions in the United States and abroad. Abstracts of the dissertations are provided. Published monthly, in several sections, since 1952. Complete copies of dissertations may be ordered from University Microfilms of Ann Arbor, Michigan.

Engineering Index

A monthly guide to the engineering literature.

Historical Abstracts

Abstracts and indexes periodicals in history, including international periodicals.

Human Resources Abstracts (formerly Poverty and Human Resources)

An abstract journal of Sage Publications providing coverage of human resource and social problems and solutions ranging from slum rehabilitation and job development training to compensatory education, minority group problems, and rural poverty.

TABLE 1.2 Continued

Index Medicus

An index of the literature in medicine, biology, and the socioeconomic aspects of disease, treatment, and health care.

Index of Economic Articles in Journals and Collective Volumes

An index of English-language articles in major professional economic journals and in collective volumes.

Index to Legal Periodicals

A guide to the literature on law and the judicial system.

INFORM

Contains abstracts of articles in over 400 English-language management and administrative science journals.

Management Contents

Contains abstracts on a wide range of business- and management-related publications, including conference proceedings.

Mental Health Abstracts

Abstracts of publications related to mental health. Sources include over 12,000 journals in 41 countries.

Personnel Management Abstracts

Provides one paragraph abstracts of selected articles and books and a more comprehensive index of authors, titles, and subjects.

Population Bibliography

Indexes journals, technical reports, government reports, and other publications related to demography.

Psychological Abstracts

Provides abstracts of articles from over 900 periodicals and 1500 books in psychology and related areas.

Sage Public Administration Abstracts

An index of publications related to public administration. Abstracts of papers are included.

Science Citation Index

Comparable to the SSCI but for the natural sciences. Includes approximately 90 percent of the significant scientific and technical literature published worldwide.

Social Sciences Citation Index (SSCI)

Indexes the significant items from approximately 1000 worldwide social and behaviorial science journals and selected articles from about 2200 journals in the natural, physical, and

(continued)

TABLE 1.2 Continued

biomedical sciences. Includes citation index, author index (first author only), and subject index. Published by the Institute for Scientific Information since 1969.

Social Science Index

A subject and author index to articles in more than 260 journals in the social and behavioral sciences, law, medicine, and related subjects.

Sociological Abstracts

Provides abstracts of selected articles from over 1200 journals in sociology and related disciplines.

United States Political Science Documents

Provides abstracts and indexing for some 150 major U.S. journals related to political science.

Work Related Abstracts

Annotated index of books, articles, and dissertations covering labor relations, personnel management, and organizational behavior.

TABLE 1.3
Published Sources: How to Get Started

Step 1: Identify what you wish to know and what you already know about your topic. This may include relevant facts, names of researchers or organizations associated with the topic, key papers and other publications with which you are already familiar, and any other information you may have.

Step 2: Develop a list of key terms and names. These terms and names will provide access to secondary sources. Unless you already have a very specific topic of interest, keep this initial list long and quite general.

Step 3: Now you are ready to use the library. Begin your search with several of the directories and guides listed in Tables 1.1 and 1.2. If you know of a particularly relevant paper or author, start with the *Social Science Citation Index* (or *Science Citation Index)* and try to identify papers by the same author, or papers citing the author or work. At this stage it is probably not worthwhile to attempt an exhaustive search. Only look at the previous two or three years of work in the area, using three or four general guides. Some directories and indices use a specialized list of key terms or descriptors. Such indices often have thesauri that identify these terms. A search of these directories requires that your list of terms and descriptors be consistent with the thesauri.

Step 4: Compile the literature you have found. Is it relevant to your needs? Perhaps you are overwhelmed by information. Perhaps you've found little that is relevant. Rework your list of key words and authors.

Step 5: Continue your search in the library. Expand your search to include a few more years and one or two more sources. Evaluate your findings.

TABLE 1.3 Continued

Step 6:   At this point you should have a clear idea of the nature of the information you are seeking and sufficient background to use more specialized resources.

Step 7:   Consult the reference librarian. You may wish to consider a computer-assisted information search. The reference librarian can assist with such a search but will need your help in the form of a carefully constructed list of key words. Some librarians will prefer to produce their own lists of key words or descriptors, but it is a good idea to verify that such a list is reasonably complete. The librarian may be able to suggest specialized sources related to the topic. Remember, the reference librarian cannot be of much help until you can provide some rather specific information about what you want to know.

Step 8:   If you have had little success or your topic is highly specialized, consult the *Directory of Directories, Directory Information Guide, Guide to American Directories, Statistics Sources* (Wasserman, O'Brien, Grace, & Clansky, 1982), *Statistical Reference Index, American Statistics Index, Encyclopedia of Geographic Information Sources* (Wasserman, Sanders, & Sanders, 1978), or one of the other guides to information listed in this book. These are really directories of directories, which means that this level of search will be very general. You will first need to identify potentially useful primary directories, which will then lead you to other sources.

Step 9:   If you are unhappy with what you have found or are otherwise having trouble, and the reference librarian has not been able to identify sources, use an authority. Identify some individual or organization that might know something about the topic. The various *Who's Who* publications, *Consultants and Consulting Organizations Directory, Encyclopedia of Associations, Industrial Research Laboratories in the United States,* or *Research Centers Directory* may help you identify sources. Don't forget faculty at universities, government officials, or business executives. Such individuals are often delighted to be of help.

Step 10: Once you have identified sources you wish to consult, you can determine whether they are readily available in your library. If they are not, ask for them through interlibrary loan. Interlibrary loan is a procedure whereby one library obtains materials from another. This is accomplished through a network of libraries that have agreed to provide access to their collections in return for the opportunity to obtain materials from other libraries in the network. Most libraries have an interlibrary loan form on which relevant information about requested materials is written. Interlibrary loans are generally made for some specific period (usually one to two weeks). Very specialized, or rare, publications may take some time to locate, but most materials requested are obtained within a couple of weeks. If you would like to purchase a particular work, consult *Ulrich's International Periodicals Directory, Irregular Serials and Annuals: An International Directory,* or *Books in Print* to determine whether a work is in print and where it may be obtained. Local bookstores often have computerized or microform inventories of book wholesalers and can provide rapid access to books and monographic items.

Step 11: Even after an exhaustive search of a library's resources, it is possible that little information will be found. In such cases, it may be necessary to identify experts

(continued)

TABLE 1.3 Continued

or other authorities who might provide the information you are seeking or suggest sources you have not yet identified or consulted. Identifying authorities is often a trial-and-error process. One might begin by calling a university department, government agency, or other organization that employs persons in the field of interest. Reference librarians often can suggest individuals who might be helpful. However, a large number of such calls may be necessary before an appropriate expert is identified.

applied setting, a familiarity with secondary sources is a prerequisite of successful practice.

The remainder of this book is concerned with getting and using secondary information. Table 1.3 provides a brief guide to getting started when seeking secondary sources.

SUMMARY

Information is a vital resource for planning and decision making. Research scientists, business planners, and government policymakers all need skills for obtaining and using information that already exists. A tremendous store of information is available, and guides, directories, and other resources are also available for identifying this information. The computer has made information increasingly accessible. There is little excuse for not using secondary data. They provide an efficient and timely place to begin any research. For many purposes, secondary data may be the only information required.

EXERCISES

Exercise 1.1: Select a topic. Following the guidelines in Table 1.3, compile a list of references, directories, authorities, and other sources of information that you would consult for further information.

Exercise 1.2: Contact several business executives, administrators, or government officials. Learn what secondary sources they routinely consult in planning and decision making. Based on what you have learned, can you identify any sources of information you think they should be consulting?

2

Evaluating Secondary Sources

Not all information obtained from secondary sources is equally reliable or valid. Information must be evaluated carefully and weighted according to its recency and credibility. When evaluating secondary information six questions must be answered: (1) What was the purpose of the study? (2) Who collected the information? (3) What information was actually collected? (4) When was the information collected? (5) How was the information obtained? (6) How consistent is the information with other sources?

The regular user of secondary information often develops a healthy skepticism about information provided by others. There are many ways that data may be misleading if they are not evaluated carefully. Data collection is usually purposive, and the purpose for which information is obtained and analyzed may influence the conclusions drawn, the data collection procedure employed, the definitions of terms and categories, and even the quality of the information. Data may become obsolete with time and lose their relevance. No data should be used without careful evaluation, and data obtained from secondary sources require especially close scrutiny.

The evaluation of secondary data should follow the same procedures employed in the evaluation of primary data. Questions concerning the source(s) of the data, measures used, the time of data collection, and the appropriateness of analyses and conclusions should be raised routinely. The questions a user of secondary sources might raise can be grouped into six broad categories:

(1) What was the purpose of the study? Why was the information collected?

(2) Who was responsible for collecting the information? What qualification, resources, and potential biases are represented in the conduct of the study?

(3) What information was actually collected? How were units and concepts defined? How direct were the measures used? How complete was the information?

(4) When was the information collected? Is the information still current or have events made the information obsolete? Were there specific events occurring at the time the data were collected that may have produced the particular results obtained?

(5) How was the information obtained? What was the methodology employed in obtaining the data?

(6) How consistent is the information obtained from one source with information available from other sources?

It is impossible to evaluate information without knowing the answers to each of these questions. One should be immediately suspicious of any information for which answers to these questions are unavailable. The importance of each of these questions is discussed in further detail in the remainder of this chapter.

WHAT WAS THE PURPOSE OF THE STUDY?

Information is rarely collected without some intent. The intent of a particular study may significantly influence the finding. Data collected to further the interests of a particular group are especially suspect. Wheeler (1977) provides an example of this problem. In 1975, the Business Roundtable commissioned a poll by Opinion Research Corporation. According to the poll, 75 percent of all Americans were opposed to the creation of a federal consumer protection agency. The question about the proposed agency asked in the poll was "Do you favor setting up an additional Consumer Protection Agency over all the others, or do you favor dong what is necessary to make the agencies we now have more effective in protecting the consumer's interests?" The question was preceded by fifteen other questions about federal agencies. The data obtained in the poll were released at the height of the debate on the creation of a federal consumer protection agency. The purpose of the study was to provide fuel for those opposed to the agency. The nature of the questions asked ensured the result sought.

Even when data are not collected for purposes of advocating a particular position, the purpose of the study may confound the interpretation of the data. The degree of precision, the types of categories used, and the method by which data are collected are often dictated by the intent of the study. The best-known measure of price movements in the United States is the Consumer Price Index (CPI) calculated monthly by the U.S. Bureau of Labor Statistics. This index is based on the prices of about 400 items of consumption. The price of each item contributing to the index is calculated by surveying wage earners and clerical workers in some base year and computing the average price paid for each item. The index represents an average for a family of four (father, 38; nonworking mother; boy, 13; and girl, 8) living in an urban area. Thus the index is not representative of the expenditures of most families. It is only a very rough index of what is happening to purchasing power and is often not useful for specific decisions where a high degree of precision is required or where expenditure patterns are different from those used to define the index.

Another example of secondary information that may not be useful for a specific question is a study carried out by the hotel industry. This study did not differentiate travelers by mode of transportation. Thus such information may be of little use to an individual interested specifically in train travel. The original purpose of the study limits its usefulness for other purposes.

WHO WAS RESPONSIBLE FOR COLLECTING THE INFORMATION?

Information from certain sources may be more credible than information from others. This arises not just from the biases that may be at work, but also from differences in technical competence, resources, and quality. Some organizations have developed reputations for high-quality control work and for the integrity of their data. Others have reputations for poor work. Generally, those sources of high integrity will provide sufficient information about how the information was obtained to enable a review of the technical adequacy of the data. Learning about the reputations of various sources of information requires investigating their previous work. Contacting clients and others who have used information supplied by the organization will also provide some indication of the reputation of an organization. One might also examine the training and expertise present in an organization supplying the information.

WHAT INFORMATION WAS ACTUALLY COLLECTED?

In the early 1950s, the Kefauver Committee published an estimate of the annual "take" from gambling in the United States. The figure, $20 billion, was actually picked at random. One committee member was quoted as saying, "We had no real idea of the money spent. The California Crime Commission said $14 billion. Virgil Peterson of Chicago said $30 billion. We picked $20 billion as the balance of the two" (Singer, 1971, p. 410). Here is an example of information entered into the public record that had no empirical basis. No data were collected at all; only a couple of opinions were sought and averaged. "Mythical numbers," as Singer (1971) refers to them, are more common than one would wish. These mythical numbers, estimates based on pure guess work, represent the extreme case, but they serve to emphasize the need for asking what information was actually collected.

Wasson and Shreve (1976) provide other examples of the necessity for identifying what information was actually collected. For example, how does one count the number of riders on a bus system? Counting the fares is not the same as counting the riders. A single rider may be represented by two or more fares, particularly when that rider is making multiple trips.

The context in which data are collected may also influence the results. Consider a study of consumer preferences that found that 60 percent of all consumers preferred brand A. Such a finding is impressive until one learns that brands B and C, the major competitors of A, were not included on the list from which consumers were to select a product.

Many of the things we wish to measure cannot be observed directly. Thus we obtain an estimate indirectly, by using a surrogate measure that is observable and assumed to be related to the more interesting phenomenon. The critical assumption of such indirect measurement techniques is that there is a relationship between the observable measure and the unobservable event of interest. Even when this assumption is correct, however, the relationship may be decidedly less than perfect. Consider studies of the success of graduates of corporate training programs. Success is difficult to measure because it involves a variety of dimensions and could be measured at many different points in time. One organization may report results using turnover during the year following completion of the training program. A second organization may use rapidity of advancement within the organization and salary increases over a three-year period. Still another organization may use ratings of success by supervisors after six months on the job. In each case, the data may be used to relate completion of the training program to success on the job. Yet the relationship reported may vary widely from one study to another. The differences in the finding are attributable to what was actually measured, the information that was actually collected. Knowing what information was actually obtained is often very useful for reconciling conflicting results. For example, it is well known that self-report data about behavior differ significantly from data about the incidence of the same behavior obtained by observation (Fiske, 1971).

Even when direct measurement is possible, the ways in which data are classified may confound the interpretations made. Categorizations and classifications may vary widely, and their relevance and meaning for a particular purpose must always be investigated. For example, what is a family? Is a single, self-supporting person, living alone a family? Are unmarried cohabitants a family? For some purposes and in some studies the answer is likely to be yes, while in other cases the answer is likely to be no. Wasson and Shreve (1976) provide an example of the problems caused by insufficient attention to the classification issue. For many years, the steel industry used total tonnage sold as its criterion of success. The criterion led the industry to overlook its losses of highly profitable low-tonnage sales to paper and aluminum products. Only too late did the industry recognize that a classification system based on uses and markets would have provided greater insight into events in its marketplace.

Wide variations in geographic, income, and age groupings across studies are quite common. There are often no accepted definitions for the concepts measured. Thus careful attention must be given to what information was actually obtained in a particular study. Apparent inconsistencies across studies often have more to do with the operational definition of terms than actual differences in the underlying phenomena.

WHEN WAS THE INFORMATION COLLECTED?

A study of the perception of the price of long-distance telephone calls found that consumers were very much aware of the price of long-distance calls and very sensitive to even small rate hikes. The results of the study might be interpreted as an indication that consumers are very price sensitive. The study, however, was carried out while an intense, highly publicized debateing over a telephone price hike raged, a debate that included several prominent politicians involved in a political campaign. It is likely that the results of the study would have been different had the study been carried out when there was less publicity about telephone rates.

Time is an important factor to be considered when evaluating information. As in the example above, factors present at the time of information collection may influence the results obtained. Time may also influence the definition of measures. For example, when is a sale made? Does the sale occur upon the placement of an order, receipt of the order, time of shipment or delivery, date of billing, date of payment, date payment is actually recorded? Different accounting systems place emphasis on different points in time and produce differences in information. Shifts in the point of time when measurements are taken may have very pronounced effects on the results obtained.

The passage of time may also change the measurement instrument. Consider the following example provided by Wasson and Shreve (1976).

In most places, the dividing line between petty and grand larceny has been $50.00 in previous generations and is now $100.00. In 1910, $50.00 represented two months' wages, while today it may represent less than two days' wages. Thus it may appear that the level of crime has increased when in fact it may have been decreasing.

Time may also make information obsolete. Data on unemployment rates in the 1960s are not particularly useful for formulating policy in the 1980s. Technological changes may change perceptions; lifestyles may change. Sooner or later most secondary data become obsolete and of interest only for historical purposes. How quickly data become obsolete depends on the type of data, the purpose for which it is used, and what new data have been obtained. The user should always know when data were collected, however, particularly since there is often a substantial time lag between data collection and the publication of results. Some data remain valid despite the passage of time, of course. For example, studies of verbal learning carried out in the 1880s remain useful even today. More recent research has added to our understanding of the learning process, however, and some conclusions have been modified as new information has been obtained.

HOW WAS THE INFORMATION OBTAINED?

The quality of secondary data cannot be evaluated without knowledge of the methodology employed when collecting the data. Information about the size and nature of samples, response rates, experimental procedures, validation efforts, questionnaires, interview guides or protocols, and analytic methods should be available in sufficient detail to allow a knowledgeable critique of the data collection procedure. The following examples help illustrate why such information is useful.

Consider a poll that finds that 80 percent of the respondents in a survey opposed gun control. One's interpretation of the 80 percent figure would be quite different if one were to learn that the sample of respondents was drawn from the membership roster of the National Rifle Association and not a representative random sample of the total population.

It has become fashionable for many periodicals to publish questionnaires for readers to complete and return. The responses are then compiled and reported in the publication. While these surveys may make entertaining reading, it is not clear to whom the results might apply. How are readers of particular publications different from the general population? One would certainly expect very different responses on certain topics from readers of *Playboy* and readers of *Christianity Today*. It is not even reasonable to generalize such results to all readers of the magazine, the people who elected to respond may differ from those who did not. Many organizations report results of surveys of their customers or clients. Such surveys may be quite useful, but indicate nothing about individuals or organizations that are not customers or clients.

The question of sampling and sample design, how people are selected for participation in a survey, is a critical issue for the evaluation of data because it deals with the question of generalizability of results. Given that a result was obtained from a particular study, can that result be considered representative of some larger population? What is the nature of that population? All too frequently one finds that it is impossible to identify that larger population. A description of the sampling procedure is always necessary when evaluating the usefulness of data. The sampling issue applies not only to people but also to other unit, such as time, organizations, locations, and situations. A more detailed description of survey and sampling procedures may be found in a companion volume in this series (Fowler, 1984).

A chronic problem with much research in the social sciences is that of missing data. Data may be missing for a variety of reasons, but the most frequent is nonresponse. When obtaining information from people, it is impossible to obtain data from everyone of interest. Individuals may not be found or they may simply refuse to cooperate. Even the Census Bureau, which is charged with collecting information about the whole population, fails to obtain 100 percent response rates. Obviously a 95 percent response rate is good and a 5 percent response rate is poor, but there are no clear guidelines for discounting information due to a low response rate. It is often helpful to know the reasons for nonresponse when evaluating information. It is also useful to compare respondents with nonrespondents on whatever information may be available for such purposes. Some information about demographic characteristics is generally obtainable and comparisons of respondents and nonrespondents should be reported for these characteristics.

Sampling and response rates are not the only details of the data collection procedure that should be available. Copies of measurement instruments, questionnaires, coding forms, and the like help identify what information was actually obtained and how it was obtained. Any experimental or field procedures employed should be described in detail. For example, in a study of consumer reactions to a new product, it would be useful to know whether the product was actually used by the consumers or whether it was simply described to them. Reports on the technical performance of products should specify the conditions under which measures were obtained. The automobile mileage estimates disseminated by the

Environmental Protection Agency (EPA) are obtained under conditions quite different from those under which most automobiles will operate.

When evaluating the procedures employed in collecting information, the critical question is one of bias. Was something done (or not done) in the study that would lead to a particular result, produce results that may not be generalizable, or confound the interpretation of the results? Such information is not always available, and when it is available, it is not always easy to obtain. When this information is available, a more useful assessment of the data provided can be done. When it is not available, a healthy skepticism is in order.

HOW CONSISTENT IS THE INFORMATION WITH OTHER INFORMATION?

When data are presented by multiple independent sources, one's confidence in that data is increased. Given all of the problems that may be present in secondary data and the frequent difficulty with identifying how the data were obtained, the best strategy is to find multiple sources of information. Ideally, two or more independent sources should arrive at the same or similar conclusions. When disagreement among sources does exist, it is helpful to try to identify reasons for such differences and to determine which source is more credible. This is not always easy, even with relatively complete information. When radically different results are reported and little basis for evaluating the information collection procedure is found, it is appropriate to be skeptical of all of the data.

A NOTE ON THE INTERPRETATION OF NUMBERS

Secondary data often come in the form of numbers. Numerical data have the appearance of being "hard" data, tangible and concrete, when compared to information presented with words. Yet a number is the ultimate abstraction, with no inherent meaning. Numbers are simply vehicles for carrying information. The user of secondary data should be comfortable with numerical data, but should also understand that numbers are no better that the information they represent and the process by which that information was generated. Unfortunately, many secondary sources do not provide the most useful numerical information.

A common means for summarizing information about trends is the use of percentages. A large proportion of government data, as well as data from other sources, are present in the percentage form. While this may be useful in some cases, it can also be misleading. Percentages are relative. A 10 percent change is quite different when the base is 100 that when it is 1,000,000. Large percentage changes often arise when computations are based on small numbers. Managers often do not understand why last year's 400 percent increase in sales has dropped to a 50 percent increase in the current year. The reason is simply one of an increasing base on which the percentage figure is calculated. Thus percentages are seldom particularly useful unless one has knowledge of their base.

A rather common method for summarizing differences among groups involves a transformation of percentages. This transformation produces an index number. Index numbers may be calculated in many ways, but all involve a comparison of two percentages. Consider the following example: Assume that 10 percent of the population as a whole owns a personal computer. Among engineers, 20 percent own personal computers, but only 1 percent of physicians own personal computers. Indices representing the likelihood of ownership of a personal computer by occupation may be constructed by dividng the percentage of ownership for each group by the percentage of ownership for the population as whole, as follows:

$$\text{index for engineers} \quad = \frac{20\%}{10\%} \ \text{x} \ \ 100 \ = \ 200$$

$$\text{index for physicians} \quad = \frac{1\%}{10\%} \ \text{x} \ \ 100 \ = \ 10$$

These numbers would be interpreted to mean the engineers as a group are twice as likely as the general population to own personal computers, while physicians are only one-tenth as likely as the general population to own personal computers. Such indices are very useful when one is trying to present information about many groups, but note that the index is the ration of two relative measures, two percentages. Thus very high indices (or very low indices) may reflect small or large bases for computation. In addition, each percentage used in the computation is itself an estimate. Consequently, the error present in an index is a combination of the errors present in the two percentages used in the computation.

Other descriptive statistics can also pose problems. Means are seldom useful without accompanying information. Generally, one would also like to have indication of the variabililty of the sample or population and the number of observations on which the mean was computed. Such information facilitates the identification of significant differences and, other things being equal, the confidence one places in the data.

SUMMARY

All data are not created equal. When using secondary sources, it is important to evaluate very carefully the information presented, to weigh potential biases, and to adopt an attitude of healthy skepticism. Conclusions should not be accepted at face value simply because they are in print or the claim is made that they are based on research. Evidence in support of conclusions must be evaluated and weight carefull to determine whether, in fact, such conclusions are justified. Alternative explanations for research findings should be identified and considered. Factors other than those identified in the study may have produced a particular result. Only careful consideration of the methods employed to collect and analyze data will reveal such alternative explanations.

Confidence in the conclusions of one study is bolstered when these conclusions are also supported in other studies. The use of multiple sources of information is, ultimately, the best defense against being misled.

EXERCISES

Exercise 2.1: The Consumer Price Index was referred to above. Reread the description of the CPI. Until recently, one assumption of the CPI was that the family of four for which the CPI is representative would purchase a new home each month. What biases are introduced by such an assumption? Who would have a vested interest in maintaining this assumption?

Exercise 2.2: A report on university students' sexual practices was published in a well-known magazine. The data were obtained from questionnaires sent in by readers of the publication. How useful are the results of the survey? What problems with this study might lead you to question the findings?

Exercise 2.3: During a municipal campaign for passage of a tax referendum, proponents of the tax increase obtained information on the tax rates of other municipalities. The conclusion drawn from these data was that, of twelve municipalities of comparable size, eleven had higher tax rates than the one in which the referendum was being held. What questions might you ask about the conclusion drawn and the data used to support this conclusion?

Exercise 2.4: A manufacturer of appliances developed an advertising campaign that emphasized the results of a survey of appliance repairmen. The results indicated that the manufacturer's products were regarded as the most reliable of all such products. However, only repairmen who serviced more than one brand of appliance were included in the survey. What questions might be raised about the study cited by the advertising?

Exercise 2.5: Several firms provide information to their subscribers about the movement of grocery products. Some firms monitor a sample of warehouses and obtain information on warehouse shipments to retailers. Others audit a sample of retail stores. Still others collect scanner checkout data where optical scanners are in use. How might these three methods of collecting data on sales volume lead to differing conclusions?

3

Government Information, Part I

Census Data

The U.S. government carries out ten censuses on a regular basis. Data from these studies are valuable for a wide range of applications. Census information is available on households, businesses, government units, transportation, and natural resources. The Census Bureau provides considerable assistance for learning about and accessing Census data. This chapter offers an introduction to Census data and its use.

The government of the United States is the world's largest gatherer of information. This "official" information is generally obtained as a by-product of administrative and regulatory functions. Such information may take the form of censuses or may be specifically commissioned studies of rather specific subjects. So great is the amount of information generated by the federal government that a single directory or guide is unavailable. Perhaps the most useful introduction to the information resources of the government is the *Guide to Federal Statistics, A Selected List* (1980). This publication of the Bureau of the Census is available from the U.S. Government Printing Office and is a guide to information directories. It describes catalogs, indices, and bibliographies of major U.S. agencies, and provides an overview of the data available from the federal government. Other publications that provide useful introductions to government information are listed in Table 3.1.

The federal government is not the only government producing information. State and local governments also produce substantial amounts of information, as do foreign governments and international organizations. Such information ranges from statistics on road use to attitudes of the general public on sex education. In the remainder of this chapter data produced by one federal agency, the Bureau of Census, will be examined; and analogous data produced by international organizations will be discussed as well. Chapter 4 will examine other types of government information.

TABLE 3.1
Publications Providing Introductions
to Federal Statistics

American Statistics Index: A Comprehensive Guide and Index to the Statistical Publications of the U.S. Government

An annual guide, with monthly supplements, to data and publications available from the federal government. Compiled by the Congressional Information Service.

Guide to U.S. Government Statistics, 7th Edition

An annotated guide covering 3200 titles in the major statistical numbered series of the U.S. government.

Statistical Abstract of the United States

A convenient statistical reference and directory to more detailed statistics reported in a variety of other government publications. Reproduces more than 1000 tables published in other Census Bureau publications, and provides a table of footnotes and a bibliography of sources. Definitions of certain categories have changed over time, making it difficult to do comparisons across time. For such analyses, the Census Bureau has published a special source book that is described below.

Historical Statistics of the United States: Colonial Times to 1970

Contains annual data on 3000 different statistical series concerning economic, social, and political life in the United States since colonial times. Consistent definitions of variables are used throughout, thus facilitating comparisons across time.

Statistics Sources (Wasserman et al., 1982)

Designed as a user's guide to statistical sources, this document provides descriptions of both government and nongovernment data sources.

THE BUREAU OF THE CENSUS

The Bureau of the Census has its origins in the U.S. Constitution, which mandates a census as the basis for apportioning representation in the U.S. House of Representatives. The earliest censuses were little more than counts of people, but over the years more and more information has been collected. Census data tend to be of very high quality and are available at a sufficient level of detail to be useful for many purposes. There are, in fact, multiple censuses today, not just one. These collect a wide range of information that is far removed from the simple "head count" mandated in the constitution. Table 3.2 provides a description of nine censuses carried out by the Bureau. The Bureau produces detailed summaries of the information it obtains and, for a nominal fee, will provide data on magnetic tapes for researchers desiring to do their own analyses (see Chapter 6). It also

TABLE 3.2
Regularly Conducted Censuses of the Bureau of the Census

Decennial Census of the Population

The Census of Population is taken every ten years, in years ending in zero. This census reports the population for states, counties, all incorporated population centers, minor civil divisions, standard metropolitan areas, and unincorporated land populated by 1000 or more individuals. It also provides detailed descriptions of subpopulations on such characteristics as sex, marital status, age, race, ethnic origin, education, family size, and relationship to the head of household. General social and economic characteristics such as mobility, state and nation of birth, number and composition of families, employment status, occupation, and income are also reported. In addition, special reports on population and housing by census tract area are provided. *Current Population Reports*, published annually, updates the information in the Census of Population based on the latest information on birthrates and death rates, migration, and so on.

Decennial Census of Housing

Data on housing are collected simultaneously with the population census. Information is provided about such characteristics as building condition, type of structure, number of occupants, number of rooms, value, monthly rent or mortgage payment, water and sewerage facilities, and equipment such as air conditioners, stoves, and dishwashers. For large metropolitan areas and certain other geographic units, data are provided at the city-block level. *Current Housing Reports* is an annual update of the Census of Housing.

Census of Business

Data are obtained every five years, in years ending in 2 and 7. The Census of Business contains statistics on retail, wholesale, and trade services by state, county, city, and type of business. Retail stores are classified by type of business, and data are provided on number of stores, total sales, and employment. Wholesalers are classified into over 150 groups, and data are provided on items such as sales volume, warehouse space, expenses, and services performed. The data provided on trade services include receipts, employment, number of units, and form of organization. *Monthly Retail Trade, Monthly Wholesale Trade*, and *Monthly Selected Services Receipts* are updates of some of the information collected in the Census of Business. The Census of Business does not include information on professions, such as law, medicine, and dentistry, nor does it provide information on the real estate and insurance industries.

Census of Manufacturers

Data are collected every fifth year, in years ending in 2 and 7. Statistics are provided on size of establishments, forms of organization, products shipped and consumed, payrolls, employment, inventories, capital expenditures, value added by manufacturer, and consumption of fuel, water, and energy. Manufacturers are categorized by type, using the approximately 450 classes in the Standard Industrial Classification System (SIC). Information is summarized by SIC code and by geographic region. The *Annual Survey of Manufacturers* provides an update of the census. Monthly and annual production figures for certain commodities are contained in *Current Industrial Reports*.

(continued)

TABLE 3.2 Continued

Census of Transportation

A national travel survey is conducted covering three major modes of transportation: passenger travel, truck and bus inventory and use, and the transport of commodities by type of carriers. The census is taken in years ending in 2 and 7. The travel information provided includes purpose, duration, origin and destination, size of party, lodgings used, and socioeconomic characteristics of travelers.

Census of Governments

Data are collected in years ending in 2 and 7. Data is obtained on the number of governmental units by state, county, and city, as well as information on government employment, elected officials, finances, taxable property values, amount of indebtedness, operating revenues and costs, and payroll.

Quinquennial Census of Agriculture

This census, taken in years ending in 4 and 9, offers data on the number of farms, types of farms, acreage, land-use practices, products and livestock raised, value of products, employment, expenditures, sources of income, and farm population by state and county. *Agriculture Statistics*, as well as numerous other publications of the Department of Agriculture, provide annual updates of selected information in the census.

Census of Mineral Industries

Data are obtained by state and nine geographic regions on size and number of mining establishments, employment, payrolls, power, and water use, equipment use, production, value of shipments, capital expenditures, type of organization, use and cost of selected supplies, and fuel and electric energy needs. This census, which is comparable to the Census of Manufacturers but for the mining industry, is taken in years ending in 2 and 7. Data are broken down for some fifty categories of industries using SIC codes. The Bureau of Mines of the Department of the Interior updates these data annually. However, the data are aggregated by product rather than by industrial classification.

Census of Construction Industries

This census provides data for 26 industries on such events as housing starts and completions, new housing authorization, payments for materials, receipts, employment, and number of firms. Data are collected in years ending in 2 and 7, and are organized both by SIC codes and geographical units. Updates of this information are published in *Current Construction Reports* and *Construction Review*.

sells computer software that may be used for accessing and tabulating data.

The quality of data obtained by the Bureau of the Census is, in part, a reflection of both the professional expertise within the Bureau and the political pressures that are brought to bear on the Bureau. The Bureau employs many highly skilled social scientists who design and execute each census. The actual data collection is carried out by mail and by paid census takers who have been carefully trained to collect information.

Although not everyone responds to the census, considerable effort is made to recontact nonrespondents in order to obtain information. In recent years, census data have taken on added importance since the federal government often allocates funds to state and local governments based on these data. Lawsuits have on occasion been filed by state and local governments because they — for whatever reason — believe that the census data represent a biased count of persons. As a result of such lawsuits, as well as general political pressures, the Bureau attempts to maintain a high-quality data collection effort that can withstand very careful scrutiny.

While the amount of data obtained by the Bureau is impressive, it is not without its drawbacks. The very size of the data collection effort, editing, coding, tabulation, and verification delay the availability of the data. It is not unusual for data to be two or more years old before they are available in report or tape form. Further compounding this lag between data collection and availability of results is the fact that censuses are not annual; they are taken every fifth or tenth year. Thus it is possible that the latest census data available may be as much as twelve years old.

A second drawback of census data is that they are not always in a form most useful for the purpose at hand. This is particularly true when data are obtained from tabulation reports of the Bureau rather than from a customized analysis of the data. Definitions of categories may not be the most appropriate for a particular use, and standard reports by geographic units are not always the most helpful approach for many analyses. These problems can often be overcome if one can obtain data tapes and develop customized analyses, however. These tapes may be ordered from the Census Bureau. The costs of such tapes reflect the Bureau's costs of producing a copy of a particulars set of data. These costs will depend on the amount of data being requested and can range upward from a few hundred dollars.

ACCESSING CENSUS DATA

The very size of the census poses problems for the researcher. The Census Bureau publishes so much information that is has become necessary for it to provide assistance to users.

There are a number of very useful guides to the census data. The *Index to Selected 1980 Census Reports* and the *Index to 1980 Census Summary Tapes* list all of the tables available from the 1980 Census by form, variables reported, and level of aggregation. Comparable guides to other censuses are also available. The Census Bureau's *Catalog of U.S. Census Publications* describes special studies and provides interim estimates; this document is published quarterly. Also available is *A Student's Work-book on the 1970 Census* (1976), which provides a tutorial on the use of census data for practical problems faced by organizations and individual researchers.

Every major metropolitan area, and many smaller cities, has at least one regional depository of federal government documents. This may be a university library or a public library. Census publications, including those identified above, are available at these depositories. In addition, selected Census Bureau publications are available at most university and public libraries. All Census Bureau publications can be purchased through the Government Printing Office.

Because many organizations, both commercial and nonprofit, make extensive use of census data for planning purposes, the Census Bureau has published *Measuring Markets: A Guide to the Use of Federal and State Statistical Data* (1979). This extremely readable and useful publication explains how census data may be applied to solve a variety of problems. *Measuring Markets* provides an overview of census data, a number of very good illustrations of how census data may be applied to specific problems, and a bibliography of additional references and data available from individual states. Two of the case illustrations in the publication are reprinted at the end of this chapter. One concerns a location problem for a new play-ground; the other regards a problem of estimating demand for a product. These illustrations provide insight into some of the types of data available from the Census Bureau and how these data may be used for solving practical problems.

Census data are available at various levels of aggregation, ranging from the smallest unit, a city block, to the entire nation. A city block is generally defined as a geographic unit bounded by four streets, but some other physical boundary, such as a river, may also be involved. Blocks are arbitrarily aggregated to form block groups, which are in turn aggregated to form census tracts. Figure 3.1 illustrates the relationship among these units of analysis. Tracts are usually defined by local communities and often, but not always, provide approximations for neighborhoods. Census tract data may be aggregated to obtain information at the county, city, or state level. Written reports of census data are not available at every level of aggregation. Data tapes must be obtained in such cases and special tabulations performed. Fortunately, a number of private firms will provide such special tabulations if the user does not find it economical to purchase data tapes and software. A number of these firms, and the services they provide, are identified in Chapter 5.

One recent innovative use of census data has combined the demographic census data with zip codes. One such system, called Potential Rating Index Zip Markets (PRIZM; see "PRIZM Adds Zips " [1980]),

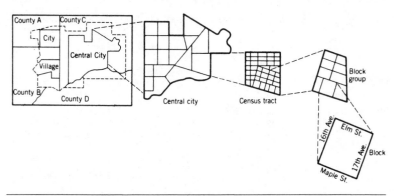

Figure 3.1:   Levels of Aggregation of the Population Census

describes each of 35,600 zip code areas along 34 demographic dimensions. These areas are then clustered into 40 groups that are very homogeneous within themselves and quite distinct from other groups with respect to demographic characteristics. The underlying assumption is that people who are similar to one another tend to live near one another. For example, one of the 40 clusters includes primarily blue-collar workers, over the age of 50, with high incomes. A second group consists of areas with many high-income families with one or more small children. The usefulness of this approach may be seen in its use by a university development office. By cross-referencing its alumni list with PRIZM areas, it was able to identify older, high-income alumni. Mailings soliciting particular types of donations to the university were directed at these individuals, making the mailing more efficient and better suited to its audience. Another use of these data would be to use the zip codes on completed product warranty cards to create profiles of purchasers.

THE STANDARD INDUSTRIAL
CLASSIFICATION SYSTEM

The Bureau of the Census has developed a uniform system of numbers for classifying organizations on the basis of their economic activities. This system is called the Standard Industrial Classification System, or SIC codes, and is the key to using census data related to economics, manufacturing, mining, and business. The classification system is widely recognized and has been incorporated into a variety of other government and proprietary information. A listing of code numbers may be found in the 1972 *Standard Industrial Classification Manual* published by the U.S. Office of Management and Budget.

TABLE 3.3
Excerpt from the Standard Industrial Classification System

Classification	SIC Code	Description
Division D: Manufacturing		
Major group	38	manufacturers of professional, scientific, and controlling instruments; photographic and optical goods; watches and clocks
Industry subgroup	381	manufacturers of engineering, laboratory, scientific, and research instruments and associated equipment
Detailed industry	3811	manufacturers of engineering, laboratory, and scientific and research instruments and associated equipment
Manufactured products	38112	manufacturers of all other laboratory and scientific instruments, excluding aircraft, nautical, and navigational instruments, and industry instruments
Manufactured	3811264	manufacturers of laboratory and scientific instruments, including medical laboratory instruments using diagnostic reagent chemicals

Reprinted by permission of the publisher from "SIC Systems and Related Data for More Effective Marketing Research," by Robert W. Haas, *Industrial Marketing Management*, Vol. 6, pp. 429-435. Copyright 1977 by Elsevier Science Publishing Co., Inc.

Table 3.3 provides an illustration of the Standard Industrial Classification System. The U.S. economy is divided into eleven major areas, such as retail trade and public administration. These major divisions are in turn broken down into industry groups identified by two-digit codes. In the illustration, SIC 38 includes all manufacturers of professional, scientific, and controlling instruments; photographic and optical goods; and watches and clocks within the manufacturing division (Division D) of the total economy. Subgroups of industries are identified by a third single-digit code. A fourth number refers to specific industries. Up to three additional digits may be used to identify specific products, making the SIC Code up to seven digits in length. Every firm or plant is given an SIC code that best describes the primary activity at its location.

Numerous organizations that provide information about industries use SIC categories. Several of these are discussed in Chapter 5. The Bureau of the Census publishes *U.S. Industrial Outlook* and *County Business Patterns,* which provide summaries and updates of information. The former publication, published annually, provides descriptions and five-year forecasts for over 200 industries.

One particularly useful set of information about industries that may be obtained from the Bureau of the Census is illustrated in Case 3.2. This is input-output information, which summarizes the flow of goods and services between sectors of the economy. This information is particularly helpful for economic and business applications, such as forecasting demand, identifying markets, and analyzing the effects of economic policy. A comprehensive treatment of input-output analysis is beyond the scope of this book, but the interested reader may refer to Bourgue (1974).

INTERNATIONAL DATA SOURCES

Many national governments collect census data similar to that obtained in the United States. For most of the developed nations of the world, data are available and reasonably accurate. Unfortunately, relatively few countries other than industrialized nations have collected data comparable to that available in the United States. Data collection in many Third World countries is either not done or is of recent origin. Data collection is improving substantially throughout the world, however. The countries themselves, as well as outside organizations (such as the United Nations), are interested in such information, and this has prompted the establishment of data collection on an international scale.

There are three critical limitations of data obtained in many countries. First, there are few data available. Until the United Nations began collecting world economics data, only rough estimates of even such fundamental statistics as population and income were available. Even in some developed nations, detailed information on industry, energy consumption, and housing may not be available or are of very recent origin.

Another problem with secondary data in other nations is a lack of reliability. Official statistics often reflect national pride and international political considerations rather than reality. One researcher (Maloney, 1976) observed that statistics in Saudi Arabia are subject to the same frequency of change "as the nation's shifting sands." Tax and trade policies within a country may provide an incentive to distort figures reported to government counters. For example, when taxes are levied on production, it is to the advantage of a firm to underreport production. The Organization for Economic Cooperation and Development (OECD) is among the older sources of international economic data and its data are among the most accurate. Yet it is frequently criticized for developing and presenting information that are consistent with the official line of its members. In the United States, reasonably reliable and valid data are readily available and are collected on a routine and (generally) timely basis. Reasonably reliable data are also available for much of Western Europe, Canada, Australia, New Zealand, and Japan. In other nations, data may be collected infrequently and on idiosyncratic schedules. Another problem is that rapid changes being experienced by many countries may quickly invalidate data. In addition, erratic scheduling of collection procedures may make it difficult to identify and follow trends. Historical data may not be defined in the same manner from occasion to occasion.

Noncomparability of data is a serious problem when one is making comparisons across information from multiple sources. National governments often differ in both the methods employed to collect data and the definiton of categories. Surveys are practical data gathering tools in literate societies, but not in others. Thus data that might be obtained directly from an individual in a literate society may have to be collected by some other means in a nonliterate society, a difference that creates some noncomparability. Also, for example, Bauer (1970) has pointed out that the United States classifies expenditures on television sets as "furniture, furnishings, and household equipment," whereas Germany classifies this expenditure as "recreation and entertainment." On most occasions, such differences do not create problems, but one should not be surprised to find them.

When seeking data on the socioeconomic characteristics of nations, a good place to begin is with the information provided by the United Nations. Table 3.4 summarizes some of the reports available through the United Nations and its affiliated agencies. A complete listing of U.N. publications may be found in the *Directory of United Nations Information Systems and Services* (1978). Another helpful document is the *Directory of International Statistics* (1975), which provides an overview of the statistical activities of the United Nations, including a listing of the statistical series compiled by the United Nations and a discussion of methodological standards.

The OECD produces numerous statistical reports and data tapes relevant to the socioeconomic characteristics of its members, as do numerous other international cooperatives. An excellent guide to much of this literature may be found in *Statistics Sources*, mentioned in Chapter 1 and described in Table 3.1.

TABLE 3.4
Selected Sources of International Demographic and Economic Data Available from the United Nations and Other Sources

Compendium of Social Statistics

Published sporadically by the United Nations. Includes basic statistical indicators describing the social situation in the world and in particular regions, as well as changes and trends in standards of living. For instance, information is provided on population size, vital statistics, heath conditions, food consumption and nutrition, housing, education and cultural activities, labor forces and conditions of employment, incomes and expenditures, and consumer prices. The most recent edition was published in 1980.

Demographic Yearbook

Published annually by the United Nations, this text is a primary source of demographic data regarding approximately 220 countries. The data describe population changes such as rate of increase, birthrates and death rates, migration, and marriages and divorces.

Index to International Public Opinion 1981-82

Published annually by Survey Research Consulting International, Inc. Contains data collected in over 100 countries. This information is obtained by the firm's own surveys as well as other surveys that may have been done. Respondents are categorized by such factors as age, sex, education, and income.

Monthly Bulletin of Statistics

A monthly publication of the United Nations reporting on population, human resources, transportation, trade, income, and finance. Provides current economic and social data for many of the tables published in the *United Nations Statistical Yearbook*.

Production Yearbook

This annual publication contains about 225 tables of data on important aspects of food and agriculture, including index numbers of agricultural and food production, food supplies, means of production, prices, freight rates, and wages throughout the world. If no official or semiofficial figures are available from a country, estimates are made by the U.N. Food and Agriculture Organization on its production of major crops, livestock, and other food products. These data are available on computer tape.

UNESCO Statistical Yearbook

Contains information on population, education, science and technology, libraries, museums, newspapers and other periodicals, book production, paper consumption, film and cinema, television and radio broadcasting, and cultural expenditures. Information is provided for over 200 countries. Published by the U.N. Educational, Scientific, and Cultural Organization.

(continued)

TABLE 3.4 Continued

United Nations Statistical Yearbook

Published annually by the United Nations since 1949, this publication provides statistics about the world regarding population, human resources, agriculture, forestry, fishing, industrial production, mining and quarrying, manufacturing, construction, energy, internal trade, external trade, transportation, communication, consumption, wages and prices, balance of payments, finance, housing, health, education, and science. *World Statistics in Brief*, available since 1976, is an annual summary of some of the most frequently used data in the *Yearbook*. Yearbooks are also available for particular world regions, such as Latin America and Asia.

World Economic Survey

This annual publication is a comprehensive review and analysis of world economic conditions and trends. Separate data are presented for developing countries, centrally planned economies, and developed market economies. Published by the United Nations.

World Health Statistics Annual

Published by the World Health Organization and the Statistical Office of the United Nations, this publication provides information on vital statistics, causes of death, infectious diseases, health personnel, and hospital establishments.

CASE 3.1

Using Census Data for Small Areas: The Location of a Playground[1]

Situation

A city parks and recreation director was recently appointed in a metropolitan area of about 100,000 people. The central city, Middletown, has about 65,000 inhabitants. The immediate task of the park director is to present a plan to the city manager for locating a new city playground in a neighborhood with a large number of children from low-income families where there are currently insufficient play areas. The playgrounds would be used most regularly by 5- to 14-year-olds. The plan must be presented to the city council with documentation for the recommendation.

What Does the Park Director Need to Know?

• Where do the playground users live in the city?
• Where are the existing playgrounds?
• Where is land available for a new playground?
• Where are the neighborhoods with large numbers of children from low-income families?

Where Should the Park Director Go to Get Her Information?

Some is available from her own office. For instance, the location of existing playgrounds is known. Therefore, on a large map of the city, she draws in the boundaries of the existing parks.

To determine where land is available, the park director goes to the city planning office and discusses the problem with the director, who shows her a map of all existing vacant land sites. The two identify several possible locations, which they then map out on a cellophane sheet to overlay on the map of existing park locations (see Figure 3.2).

The park director still needs to know where in the city low-income families with children live. The city planner suggests she consult the 1980 Census data to obtain this information. The census reports average ages and incomes of city residents living in neighborhoodlike areas called "census tracts." The planner explains that this information can be found in the Census Tract Report. In the top left corner of the report is the code "PHC(1)," which references this series of census reports. The P and H together in the code indicate that the report includes data from both the population and housing censuses.

They open the PHC(1) report and look at the table that gives age data for both males and females (referred to as "age by sex") for the entire county, the city, the remainder of the county ("balance"), and the individual census tracts. Studying the table further, they see that two lines are labeled "Male, 5 to 9 years" and "Male, 10 to 14 years" with the equivalent lines for females. The park director simply needs to add the columns on the office adding machine to obtain the total number of children aged 5-14 living in these areas.

They then turn to the back of the report, where there is a map showing the boundaries of the census tracts and the tract numbers referred to in the census tables. Next, from the table of contents, they identify a table titled "Income Characteristics of the Population: 1980." This table shows the income distribution and other data on individuals earning "income below the poverty level." The poverty index provides a range of low-income cutoffs with adjustments for family size, sex of the family head, number of children under age 18, and farm versus nonfarm residency.

The income characteristic of each tract can be described in any of the following ways:

(1) an income distribution

(2) the mean or median income

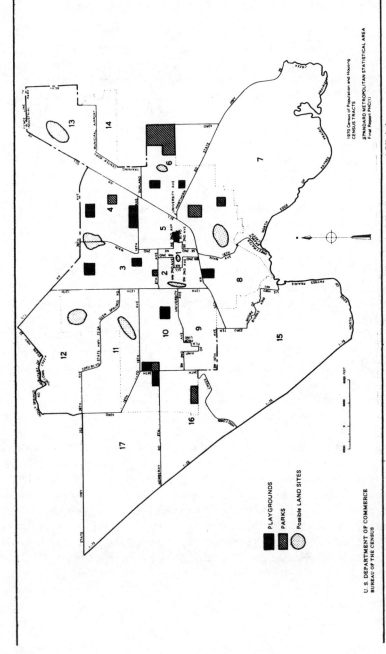

Figure 3.2: Existing Playgrounds, Parks, and Possible Land Sites, 1971: Census Tracts in Middletown and Vicinity

(3) the number of families whose incomes are from public assistance or public welfare

(4) percentage of families with a ratio of family income to the poverty level of less than 1.0

(5) the number of families with incomes below the poverty level

(6) the number of families with incomes below the poverty level and with children under the age of 18

The park director studies each possibility in light of her particular needs. She must first decide on a definition of "low-income." She can use the 1980 Census poverty index or her own operational definition using the income data in options 1-5 above. However, if she selects from options 1-5, she can only find areas with a high concentration of low-income families, but she will not know whether children are present (a recommendation to place a playground in a predominantly low-income elderly neighborhood would not win the park director a promotion!). Therefore, she must also choose option 6, which is a count of families with children under 18 whose family incomes are below the poverty level. She cannot directly determine the number of 5- to 14-year-olds from this summary. Thus she has the following choices:

(1) Use the counts of low-income families with children under 18 combined with counts of children aged 5-14. Then make an approximation of the number of 5- to 14-year-olds in low-income families. Such an approximation can be made by multiplying the mean number of such children by the number of low-income families with children. Then, using the age data for the total population, compute the proportion of the under-18 population that is 5 to 14 years old and, finally, the proportion of these children living in low-income families. The Appendix to this case study illustrates this method of approximation. Note that the mean number of children in a family varies considerably, and that, therefore, a decision based solely on the number of families might be misleading.

(2) Get the data in the exact form desired by requesting "special tabulation" from the Census Bureau. The park director called the Census Bureau for a rough estimate and found that a special tabulation would cost about $3000. She decided that in this particular case it was not worth the expense of a special tabulation. With the aid of a calculator, she filled in the computation sheet shown in Table 3.5 to estimate the number of children aged 5-14 in low-income families. As she developed the computation sheet, she noticed that tracts, 6, 7, 8, 11, 12, 14, 16, and 17 had data listed in three places; "Middletown," the "balance of county," and "totals for split tracts." That is, these split tracts cross the city boundaries and thus separate data are given for the part of the tract in the city of Middletown, the part outside the city (balance columns), and the total for the

TABLE 3.5
Computation of an Approximation of the Number of Children Aged 5-14 in Low-Income Families in Middletown: 1970

Tract No.	(1) No. Children Under 18 In Low-Income Families[a]	(2) Total No. 5-14 Year Olds	(3) Total No. Under 18 Years	(4) Pop. Aged 5-14 Pop. Under 18	(5) Est. No. Children Aged 5-14 in Low- Income Families
Total SMSA	7137[b]	18861	32923	0.57	4068
Middletown	3699	10098	17922	0.56	2071
0001	—	67[c]	123	.54	—
0002	(2.65)(221) = 586	621	1140	.54	316
0003	(2.49)(70) = 174	797	1486	.54	94
0004	(2.17)(35) = 76	1360	2286	.59	45
0005	(2.12)(77) = 163	705	1267	.56	91
0006	(3.46)(231) = 799	1053	1779	.59	471
0007	(3.21)(391) = 1255	1602	2726	.59	740
0008	(1.82)(33) = 60	174	395	.44	26
0009	(1.60)(159) = 254	231	820	.28	71
0010	(1.85)(39) = 72	793	1370	.58	42
0011	—	478	810	.59	—
0012	(2.76)(51) = 141	397	762	.52	73
0013	—	550	820	.67	—
0014	—	4	6	.66	—
0016	(2.00)(43) = 86	708	1169	.61	52
0017	—	558	963	.58	—

a. These do not add to 3699 because of suppression in tracts 0001 and 0017.
b. Middletown plus the balance do not add to 7137 because of rounding.
c. As an example of this calculation: 67 = 17 + 13 + 8 + 29.

entire tract. For this study, she used only the data for the Middletown sections of the tracts.

The city planner discussed some aspects of the data of which the user should be aware:

The census was taken in April of 1980. After several years, the characteristics of populations change, especially in small geographic areas, as people age and move in and out of the area. Lacking a source of more recent data, the park director can only assume that the relationships among the tracts are relatively the same as they were in 1980. Census data can never be viewed as exact. In any mass statistical operation such as a decennial census, human and mechanical errors occur, although efforts are made to keep these nonsampling errors at an acceptably low level. Also, some data are based on a sample and thus are subject to sampling errors as well.

Sometimes data are omitted and replaced by ellipses in the data tables. This occurs when (1) the number of people in a certain category is so small that it might be possible to identify them if the information were released, and thus the data are withheld to maintain confidentiality; or (2) when the base of a derived figure (such as a median or percentage) is too small to provide reliable data, and therefore the statistics are not computed to maintain data quality.

It is also important to recognize that the computations carried out are based on the following assumptions:

(1) The census gives us information based on poverty level. The computations assume that "low income" and the "poverty level" are the same thing. However, it could be argued that this understates the number of low-income people, since people above the poverty level can still earn very low incomes. The question then is whether these low-income people who are above the poverty level are living in different areas than those below the poverty level. Results could change if this is so.

(2) The computations also assume that the proportion of 5- to 14-year-old children in the population of children under 18 (that is, column 4 of Table 3.5) is the same for poverty-level families as families at other income levels. If this is not so, again the results might be misleading.

(3) A fundamental question is which age group will use the playground the most. These computations assume that children between the ages of 5 and 14 all use playgrounds with equal frequency.

(4) Finally, the data refer to one point in time. Therefore, planners using the data can only assume that they reflect future population characteristics.

The results of the computations in Table 3.5 indicate that only three tracts are serious prospects for the playground (assuming validity of the numbers). These are:

tract number	estimated number of children 5-14 in low-income families
0007	740
0006	471
0002	361

These results must then be compared with the current playground, parks, and possible land sites given in Figure 3.2. This examination indicates the following:

(1) Tract 7 has a land site, but already has two parks.
(2) Tract 6 has a land site, but already has two playgrounds.
(3) Tract 2 has a land site and no parks or playground. There is a playground in tract 5 not far from tract 2; however, it is a good bet to be across many busy streets from tract 2 and thus not very accessible.

The appropriate choice is also related to whether one assumes that a park is a substitute for a playground. If it is not, tract 7 appears best. If it is, then tract 2 appears best suited.

Appendix:
Computational Illustration

Data are not always published in the exact form desired, but it is often possible to compute what is needed. In this case study, for example, the park director wanted an approximation of the number of 5- to 14-year-olds in low-income families. The description below illustrates a method for doing this if you are willing to assume that the proportion of children 5-14 is the same in the total population as it is in the low-income family population. (The steps below relate to the columns in Table 3.5.)

(1) Compute the number of related children under 18 in the low-income families:

Column 1 = (mean number of related children under 18 years) (number of families with income below the poverty level with related children under 18 years)

For the SMSA, this is: (2.88) (2,478) = 7,137

(2) Compute the total population age 5-14 years:

Column 2 = (males 5 to 9 years) + (males 10 to 14 years) + (females 5 to 9 years) + (females 10 to 14 years)

For the SMSA, this is 4,809 + 4,791 + 4,588 + 4,673 = 18,861

(3) The number of persons under 18 years is shown under the heading "Type of Family and Number of Own Children."

For the SMSA, the number of persons under 18 years is 32,923.

(4) Compute the proportion of the total 0-17 population that is 5-14 years:

$$\text{Column 4} = \frac{\text{column 2}}{\text{column 3}}$$

For the SMAS, this is: $\dfrac{18,861}{32,923}$ = 0.57

(5) Compute an estimate of the number of 5- to 14-years-olds in low-income families:

Column 5 = (column 4) (column 1)

For the SMSA, this is: (0.57) (7,137) = 4,068

CASE 3.2

Unlimited Data Research Company

Objective

To predict the potential market in 1983 to sell paper and allied products to merchant wholesalers and in retail trade.

Kind of Business

A research company engaged in economic studies, industrial development, and marketing research.

Problem

The research company was engaged by a paper manufacturer to estimate the market potential for paper and allied products to merchant wholesalers and in retail trade. First, since the manufacturer had sales representatives and needed to determine its sales force, it wanted to know the quantity of paper and allied products consumed directly by various trades. Second, the research company was asked to project total 1983 requirements, both direct and indirect, of wholesale and retail trade. Finally, the research organization was requested to project the manufacturer's share of the market, given the fact that, based on past history, the manufacturer normally account for 15 percent of the total market for paper and allied products.

Source of Data

(1) "Input-Output Structure of the U.S. Economy 1967," *Survey of Current Business* (February 1974).

(2) 1979 *U.S. Industrial Outlook* (with projections to 1983).

Assumptions

(1) The relative demand for paper and allied products by wholesale and retail trades will remain the same in 1983 as in 1982.

(2) To compute both direct and indirect use of paper and allied products by wholesale and retail trade, the research company used gross profit, or gross margin, which it estimated to be almost 25 percent of sales. To demonstrate the links between producing and consuming industries and the effect on final markets in the input-output tables, commodities are shown as if moving directly from producer to user, bypassing trade. Therefore, the output of trade is measured in terms of total margins, that is, operating expenses plus profits.

Procedure

According to the 1979 U.S Industrial Outlook (source 2), merchant wholesaler sales in 1983 will be $1200 billion and retail sales should be about $1200 billion. The combined total in 1983 will therefore be $2400 billion.

Since the manufacturer wanted to know the amount of paper and products consumed directly by wholesale and retail trade, the research company first computed 25 percent (gross profit) of $2400 billion, which came to $600 billion. Then, from Table 3.6 (which was reproduced from Table 2 of the input-output study in source 1), it found that, for each dollar of gross profit of wholesale and retail trade, $0.006 worth of paper was consumed directly. Therefore, the total amount consumed directly by the wholesale and retail trades was $3.6 billion (600 billion x $0.006). This represents only the cost of paper products that are used directly by the two trades and does not include products used indirectly by the manufacturers of food and kindred products or by nonfood merchandise that is distributed via the wholesale and retail trades method.

In addition, the research company computed estimates of total requirements of paper and allied products including those used by processors of other materials consumed by manufacturers. This was measured by using the direct and indirect costs shown in Table 3.7 (reproduced from Table 3 of the input-output study) and was found to be $0.015. Thus total requirements in 1983 were estimated to be $9 billion ($600 billion x $0.015).

The paper manufacturer reported that its share of the total market for paper and allied products to the wholesale and retail trades was 15 percent. The research company therefore projected the manufacturer's share of the total market to be $1350 million ($9 billion x 15 percent).

TABLE 3.6

Direct Requirements per Dollar of Gross Output, 1967

Industry No.	For the composition of inputs to an industry, read the column for that industry	Communications, except radio and TV broadcasting 66	Radio and TV broadcasting 67	Electric, gas, water and sanitary services 68	Wholesale and retail trade 69	Finance and insurance 70
1	Livestock and livestock products				.00006	
2	Other agricultural products					
3	Forestry and fishery products					
4	Agricultural, forestry and fishery services				.00085	
5	Iron and ferroalloy ores mining			.00001	(*)	
6	Nonferrous metal ores mining			.00002		
7	Coal mining	0.00002	0.00009	.02399	(*)	0.00003
8	Crude petroleum and natural gas			.06756	.00002	
9	Stone and clay mining and quarrying			(*)	.00003	
10	Chemical and fertilizer mineral mining			(*)		
11	New construction					
12	Maintenance and repair construction	.02934	.00195	.03047	.00322	.00282
13	Ordnance and accessories			.00001	.00023	
14	Food and kindred products			.00004	.00546	
15	Tobacco manufactures			.00001	.00006	
16	Broad and narrow fabrics, yarn and thread mills			.00005	.00012	
17	Miscellaneous textile goods and floor coverings			.00018	.00033	
18	Apparel			.00022	.00082	
19	Miscellaneous fabricated textile products	.00027			.00049	
20	Lumber and wood products, except containers			.00002	.00056	
21	Wooden containers				.00065	
22	Household furniture			(*)	.00015	
23	Other furniture and fixtures				.00016	
24	Paper and allied products, except containers	.00110	.00013	.00091	.00616	.00525
25	Paperboard containers and boxes	.00001	.00006	.00008	.00350	
26	Printing and publishing	.00210	.00031	.00020	.00232	.00932
27	Chemicals and selected chemical products	.00003		.00150	.00132	.00002
28	Plastics and synthetic materials			.00006	.00015	
29	Drugs, cleaning and toilet preparations			(*)	.00168	
30	Paints and allied products	.00005	.00003	.00001	.00031	
31	Petroleum refining and related industries	.00336	.00016	.00737	.00842	.00192
32	Rubber and miscellaneous plastics products	.00123	.00016	.00061	.00437	.00028
33	Leather tanning and industrial leather products			(*)	.00001	
34	Footwear and other leather products				.00024	
35	Glass and glass products				.00079	
36	Stone and clay products	.00001		.00002	.00097	
37	Primary iron and steel manufacturing			.00109	.00023	
38	Primary nonferrous metal manufacturing	.00052		.00029	.00026	
39	Metal containers				.00066	
40	Heating, plumbing and structural metal products			(*)	.00110	

SOURCE: *Survey of Current Business* (February 1974).
* Less than $500,000 input.

TABLE 3.7

Total Requirements (Direct and Indirect) per Dollar of Delivery to Final Demand, 1967

Each entry represents the output required, directly and indirectly, from the industry named at the beginning of the row for each dollar of delivery to final demand by the industry named at the head of the column.

Industry No.		Transportation and warehousing 65	Communications; except radio and TV broadcasting 66	Radio and TV broadcasting 67	Electric, gas, water and sanitary services 68	Wholesale and retail trade 69	Finance and insurance 70
1	Livestock and livestock products	0.00341	0.00147	0.00918	0.00169	0.00502	0.00388
2	Other agricultural products	.00368	.00133	.01341	.00170	.00418	.00335
3	Forestry and fishery products	.00037	.00020	.00043	.00032	.00043	.00040
4	Agricultural, forestry and fishery services	.00040	.00018	.00184	.00027	.00130	.00038
5	Iron and ferroalloy ores mining	.00086	.00019	.00022	.00055	.00031	.00019
6	Nonferrous metal ores mining	.00058	.00023	.00025	.00043	.00028	.00018
7	Coal mining	.00163	.00060	.00120	.03657	.00124	.00117
8	Crude petroleum and natural gas	.02414	.00174	.00464	.09534	.00772	.00439
9	Stone and clay mining and quarrying	.00097	.00059	.00047	.00139	.00055	.00040
10	Chemical and fertilizer mineral mining	.00036	.00012	.00024	.00044	.00028	.00022
11	New construction	.04070	.03341	.01697	.07628	.01269	.01316
12	Maintenance and repair construction	.00032	.00018	.00019	.00010	.00037	.00010
13	Ordnance and accessories						
14	Food and kindred products	.00859	.00166	.01744	.00385	.01350	.00978
15	Tobacco manufacturers	.00021	.00021	.00103	.00021	.00044	.00056
16	Broad and narrow fabrics, yarn and thread mills	.00284	.00079	.00087	.00134	.00223	.00118
17	Miscellaneous textile goods and floor coverings	.00172	.00031	.00045	.00071	.00106	.00053
18	Apparel	.00091	.00057	.00036	.00070	.00138	.00032
19	Miscellaneous fabricated textile products	.00226	.00118	.00025	.00031	.00080	.00025
20	Lumber and wood products, except containers	.00276	.00166	.00151	.00308	.00344	.00284
21	Wooden containers	.00010	.00006	.00013	.00006	.00077	.00007
22	Household furniture	.00012	.00023	.00013	.00008	.00023	.00005
23	Other furniture and fixtures	.00010	.00004	.00004	.00007	.00022	.00004
24	Paper and allied products, except containers	.00717	.00604	.00677	.00544	.01549	.02214
25	Paperboard containers and boxes	.00203	.00074	.00147	.00104	.00517	.00143
26	Printing and publishing	.01044	.01339	.01786	.00840	.01838	.04696
27	Chemicals and selected chemical products	.00892	.00311	.00709	.01132	.00762	.00563
28	Plastics and synthetic materials	.00319	.00122	.00151	.00196	.00270	.00165
29	Drugs, cleaning and toilet preparations	.00105	.00071	.00120	.00108	.00271	.00133
30	Paints and allied products	.00334	.00151	.00102	.00325	.00119	.00081
31	Petroleum refining and related industries	.05030	.00655	.00597	.01846	.01343	.00675
32	Rubber and miscellaneous plastics products	.00941	.00312	.00314	.00403	.00748	.00352
33	Leather tanning and industrial leather products	.00007	.00006	.00014	.00005	.00014	.00009
34	Footwear and other leather products	.00012	.00019	.00051	.00010	.00042	.00020
35	Glass and glass products	.00174	.00057	.00103	.00073	.00153	.00052
36	Stone and clay products	.00288	.00163	.00136	.00412	.00233	.00110
37	Primary iron and steel manufacturing	.01673	.00356	.00197	.01016	.00582	.00355
38	Primary nonferrous metal manufacturing	.00822	.00340	.00134	.00536	.00361	.00231
39	Metal containers	.00087	.00040	.00082	.00062	.00150	.00086
40	Heating, plumbing and structural metal products	.00311	.00204	.00119	.00495	.00213	.00094

SOURCE: *Survey of Current Business* (February 1974).

Conclusion

Based upon projected demand for paper and allied products by the trades, the manufacturer drafted a proposed plan for enlarging the plant, adding more salespersons, redefining sales territories, and expanding other facets of business operations.

EXERCISES

Exercise 3.1: What sources of information provided by the U.S. Bureau of the Census would you consult for data on the energy consumption patterns of households and organizations in a particular county?

Exercise 3.2: Find the most recent report of the Census of Manufacturers. For your county, identify the number of firms that are engaged in the manufacture of household furniture (SIC 251), power equipment (SIC 34433, and 35111), and industrial organic chemicals (SIC Code 2865). How many banking firms (SIC 602) are there in your county? What industry is the largest in your county in terms of number of employees? In terms of sales?

Exercise 3.3: Your local city government is considering opening a group of daycare centers for elderly citizens. Using only secondary data, assess the demand for such centers and identify potential sites for locating such centers.

Exercise 3.4: Identify the demographic characteristics of leisure travelers in the United States who do the most traveling.

Exercise 3.5: What nations of the world are in the greatest need of assistance with increasing crop production per acre?

NOTES

1. This case is an adaptation of a case prepared by Cynthia Murray Taeuber of the U.S. Bureau of the Census. Used with permission.

2. This case is reprinted by permission of the U.S. Department of Commerce, Industry and Trade Administration, from *Measuring Markets: A Guide to the Use of Federal and State Statistical Data* (1979).

4

Government Information, Part II

Other Government Documents

A wide range of data, information, and statistics is provided by government agencies other than the Census Bureau. Federal, state, and local government agencies, the judicial system, and legislative bodies produce vast quantities of highly reliable information. International agencies, such as the United Nations, provide information about nations other than the United States and about global issues. This chapter discusses these sources of data and means for identifying and accessing this information.

The Bureau of the Census is only one of the many federal agencies that generate reports, data, and other types of information. Indeed, despite the volume of census data, it represents only a fraction of the information issued by federal government agencies. The Freedom of Information Act of 1966 opens numerous sources of data to public scrutiny that otherwise would be unavailable. Under the act, administrative agencies in the executive branch of the federal government must release any identifiable records unless the information falls within one of the nine exemption categories. A discussion of the procedure for obtaining information under the Freedom of Information Act is provided later in this chapter.

Not all information generated by governmental bodies is collected and reported as carefully as are census data. Government agencies are frequently prone to find answers to questions, no matter how unrealistic, rather than admit to not knowing. A widely quoted figure on the cost of air pollution was apparently based on a single study in Pittsburgh early in the century (Wasson, 1974). This figure was extrapolated to a national level and submitted in a report to Congress. Generally, the most reliable government information is that generated by regularly scheduled surveys and studies. A number of agencies publish regular statistical reports, including those listed below.

AGENCIES THAT PUBLISH REPORTS

The Federal Reserve System

The Federal Reserve System issues a monthly publication, the *Federal Reserve Bulletin*. This publication reports statistics on banking, security markets, various financial data (consumer, business, government, and real estate), international money rates, savings, flow of funds, income, national product, department store sales, and international trade data. The *Federal Reserve Chart Book*, issued quarterly, and *Historical Chart Book*, issued annually, also provide a variety of data on financial statistics and consumer buying.

Department of Agriculture

The Department of Agriculture (DOA) publishes three major volumes each year: *Agricultural Statistics*, *Crop Production*, and *Crop Values*. These three publications provide information on the number and type of farm operations, the quantity of production of various crops and livestock, and the real and expected values of particular crops. The DOA also publishes monthly reports and numerous special studies. *Foreign Agricultural Trade of the United States*, published monthly, provides data on the value and quantity of imported and exported agricultural commodities. These reports are widely used by economists, rural sociologists, and government and business planners.

Department of Labor

The Labor Department conducts detailed studies of family expenditure patterns in order to update the Consumer Price Index. These studies are carried out regularly and the results published. The department also publishes the *Monthly Labor Review*. This review contains statistics on employment and unemployment; labor turnover; wages and hours worked; work stoppages; retail, wholesale, and commodity price indexes; and other current labor statistics. The *Directory of Occupational Titles*, published sporadically by the Department of Labor, contains reports of job analyses of over 20,000 occupations. This document includes information about activities and trade requirements of relatively standardized jobs. The Bureau of Labor Statistics within the department makes projections of labor market conditions and future occupation supply, by occupation. These data are widely used for human resources planning and for developing and implementing employment policies.

Employment and Earnings Statistics for States and Areas is an annual publication of over 7500 statistical series on payroll employment by industry. It also reports 3300 series on hours and earnings of production workers by industry. All available data for the given time period are reported. Information is broken down by state and by 202 major areas. A companion volume, *Employment and Earnings Statistics for the United States*, is an annual summary at the national level. Two monthly publications, *Employment and Earnings* and *Monthly Report on the Labor Force*, provide updates. The *Directory of Data Sources on Racial and Ethnic Minorities* organizes and describes the economic, demographic, and social data published by the federal government that is pertinent to minorities. Finally, the *Handbook of Labor Statistics* and *BLS Handbook of Methods*, published by the Bureau of Labor Statistics, provide information on prices, cost of living, earnings, hours worked, wage rates, and so on.

Department of Commerce

In addition to the substantial output of the Bureau of the Census, the Department of Commerce produces numerous studies and reports. It publishes the *Survey of Current Business* each month. This document contains over 2000 statistical series covering such information as commodity prices, construction and real estate, general business indicators, domestic trade, employment, population, finance, transportation, communications, and international transactions. *Business Conditions Digest* is designed to serve as a general guide to economic conditions. It contains 70 indicators of business and is published monthly by a unit of the Census Bureau. Another specialized publication of the Bureau of the Census is the *County and City Data Book*. Published every two years, it provides a convenient source of statistics on a city and county basis, including population, income, education, employment, and housing. *Business Statistics* is published every two years and provides a historical record of the data series reported in the monthly *Survey of Current Business*. This latter publication provides a comprehensive statistical summary of national income and product accounts in the United States. Over 2600 different statistical series are reported. *County Business Patterns* is a joint publication of the Departments of Commerce and Health and Human Services. It contains statistics on the number and types of businesses by county. It also provides information on employment and payroll. *Social Indicators* presents data on major social trends in population, health, education, employment, income, housing, leisure, social mobility, and public safety.

A special division of the Department of Commerce, the National Technical Information Service (NTIS), collects and disseminates technical report information generated by government-funded research. NTIS maintains a databank of 250,000 abstracts of federally sponsored technical reports published since 1964. Customized bibliographic services are available. NTIS also distributes a bibliography of translations on significant research literature in other languages. NTIS publishes the *National Environmental Statistical Report*, which summarizes environmental data and trends. Finally, *Ethnic Statistics: A Compendium of Reference Sources* abstracts 92 federal statistical data resources that contain ethnic or racial data. A users' guide, *Ethnic Statistics: Using National Data Resources for Ethnic Studies*, is also available.

Department of Education

The Department of Education publishes an annual *Digest of Educational Statistics*. This publication provides data on student populations, the teaching force, schools, colleges and universities, vocational schools, and other information relevant to educational policy. *Projections of Educational Statistics* describes trends during the past ten years and provides forecasts for the next ten years.

Department of Health and Human Services

The Department of Health and Human Services publishes the monthly *Vital Statistics Report* and an annual summary volume, *Vital Statistics in the United States*. These publications provide information on births, deaths, marriages, and a variety of statistics related to health.

Council of Economic Advisers

The monthly publication, *Economic Indicators*, is published by this agency. The publication includes charts and tables with general economic data related to personal consumption expenditures, gross national product, and so on. The council also compiles an annual report that reviews economic policy and provides forecasts. This annual report is a part of the *Economic Report of the President*.

Economic Statistics Bureau

The *Handbook of Basic Economic Statistics* is published annually, with monthly supplements. It is a compilation of statistics regarding the national economy collected by federal agencies. A complete historical series is provided for each statistic reported.

Internal Revenue Service

Statistics of Income is published annually by the Internal Revenue Service. The information in these volumes is taken from the annual federal income tax returns of corporations and individuals. There are actually several different publications, each relevant to a different type of tax return: individual, corporate, partnership, or proprietorship.

Bureau of Economic Analysis

The Bureau of Economic Analysis (BEA) publishes a monthly analysis of economic indicators entitled *Business Conditions Digest*. Each issue has two parts: (1) "cyclical indicators," which includes cyclical indicators for various economic processes; composite indices of economic activity; and indices of diffusion and rates of change; and (2) "other important economic measures," which includes data on the labor force; employment and unemployment; government involvement in business activities, prices, wages, and productivity; national income; and international transactions. BEA's *Handbook of Cyclical Indicators* is a helpful guide to using this publication.

A second useful BEA publication is the monthly *Defense Indicators*. This publication carries some sixty statistical time series on defense activities. Included are information on expenditures, contracts, orders, obligations, shipments, inventories, employment, and earnings.

Local Area Personal Income 1971-76 provides a breakdown of personal income by major industry, population, and per capita for states, counties, and regions. *Long Term Economic Growth 1860-1970* presents a comprehensive, long-term perspective on the U.S. economy.

National Criminal Justice Information and Statistics Service

The *Source Book for Criminal Justice Statistics*, published annually, reports recent criminal justice data and some historical data.

Federal Bureau of Investigation

The annual publication *Uniform Crime Reports for the United States* presents data on crime rates, trends, public safety, arrests, and employment. *Uniform Crime Reporting* is a quarterly update of these data.

Federal Communications Commission

Statistics of the Communications Industry in the U.S. is an annual report of financial and operating data concerning telephone, wire-telegraph, ocean-cable, and radiotelegraph carriers and companies. It also provides information on employment, compensation, and numbers of telephones by states and principal cities.

Department of Energy

The Energy Information Administration (EIA) publishes a semiannual guide to the data contained in publications of the EIA. *EIA Data Index: An Abstract Journal* and a companion publication, *EIA Publications Directory: A User's Guide*, are good introductions to the vast quantity of data collected by the Department of Energy. These data include actual and projected energy resource reserves, consumption, production, prices, supply and demand, and other information about U.S. energy production and use.

Department of Housing and Urban Development

The *Housing and Urban Development Statistical Yearbook* provides a detailed and comprehensive set of statistical information on housing and urban development. Some of the data reported were collected by the department; however, information obtained by other government agencies and private organizations is also included.

Securities and Exchange Commission

The Securities and Exchange Commission (SEC) collects volumes of information on individual corporations in the United States. This source is a good place to begin researching any domestic company selling stocks to the public. Documents may be obtained by mail for a nominal cost. Many libraries carry selected SEC documents. Among the more useful SEC documents are the following forms and reports filed by companies: 10-K, 10-Q, and 8-K.

Form 10-K, which is filed annually, includes information on the type of business the company is in, number of employees, estimates of competitors, names of executive officers and directors, locations of properties owned, changes in competitive conditions and product lines, research and development expenditures, patents and trademarks, sales, revenues, profits, income, and total assets. Forms 10-Q and 8-K provide updates for Form 10-K between filings. All of these forms provide a wealth of information about individual companies. A reasonably comprehensive picture of an industry can often be constructed by examining the 10-Ks of the competing companies. These forms may be obtained by requesting the specific form, for a particular filing period, for the corporation(s) of interest. Such data are often quite useful to economists studying specific industries, and to business planners interested in competitors.

Central Intelligence Agency

The *Handbook of Economic Statistics* provides data on all Communist and selected non-Communist countries. Topics included are economic performance, aid, agriculture, foreign trade, energy, and related topics.

National Science Board

Science Indicators presents data on public attitudes toward science and technology, science and engineering personnel, resources for basic research, industrial research and development, and international research.

Congressional Information Service

The *Statistical Reference Index* is a selective guide to statistics and data compiled by organizations other that the federal government. It is published monthly. The *American Statistics Index: A Comprehensive Guide and Index to the Statistical Publications of the U.S. Government* is a monthly guide to the statistical publications of the federal government.

General Accounting Office

Among the publications of the General Accounting Office is *Federal Evaluations*. This publication, last issued in 1980, describes over 2000 program and management evaluations carried out by federal government agencies. It is not published regularly.

State and Local Governments

The federal government is not the only governmental source of information. State and local government units also obtain substantial data on topics relevant to their concerns. States often publish statistical abstracts. In addition, the *Encyclopedia of Geographic Information Sources* (Wasserman et al., 1978) is a useful guide to periodicals, directories, and statistics about states and cities. Finally, data regarding automobile registrations, business licenses, marriages, and the like are generally tabulated by states and local governments and are available in one form or another.

The Courts

Records of the judiciary system are often open to the public, although this is not always the case. In federal and state courts, records are available from the court clerk's office. Each office maintains a judgment index that lists cases by plaintiff and defendant. The Supreme Court maintains a library, and there are regional depositories of court records throughout the country. Local court clerks' offices can usually assist in identifying the nearest regional depository.

Information on Government Grants,
Contracts, and Assistance

Frequently individuals are interested in learning about opportunities for supplying services to the government or obtaining assistance from government agencies. Academic researchers and institutions frequently want information on grants for research or training. Local and regional government bodies often wish to learn of federal assistance programs. Business firms are interested in contract work, bids for equipment, and other commercial transactions of the federal government. A particularly useful guide to such information is the *United States Government Manual*, an official handbook of the federal government. The *Manual* contains descriptions of all federal agencies and their activities. A special section of the *Manual* is called "Guide to Government Information," and explains how to keep in touch with U.S. government publications.

The sheer magnitude of federal programs necessitated the publication of a guide to assistance programs. *The Catalog of Federal Domestic Assistance (CFDA)* is a comprehensive listing of federal programs and activities providing assistance or benefits to the public. Information on a wide range of programs is provided in the *CFDA*, ranging from grants and loans to insurance.

Persons or firms desiring to sell to the federal government should become familiar with the *Commerce Business Daily (CBD)*. *CBD*, published by the Department of Commerce, is the means by which the federal government announces opportunities to bid on the procurement of equipment, materials, services, contract research, and the like. Department of Defense projects expected to cost at least $10,000, and other departmental or agency projects expected to cost at least $5,000, must be advertised in *CBD*. Announcements of contracts and awards are also published.

The *Federal Register* is a daily publication of the federal government. The *Register* announces newly proposed programs, recently adopted regulations, and changes in existing programs and policies. The *Federal Register* is of particular importance to social science researchers because it makes grant announcements. Individual agencies often have their own publication vehicles as well. For example, the National Instututes of Health publish *NIH Research Contracting Process* and *Guide to Grant and Award Programs*. The National Endowment for the Arts publishes *Cultural Directory: Guide to Federal Funds and Services for Cultural Activities*.

A rather substantial industry has grown up to monitor government programs. For fees, ranging from modest to quite high, various members of this industry will provide information on specific government programs. Several firms now provide online computer search capabilities that allow one to identify information relevant to a particular agency program quickly (see Chapter 6). One particularly useful publication of this type is the *Annual Register of Grant Support*, published by Marquis Who's Who. This publication is the only annually revised directory of sources of financial assistance. It includes not only government programs but also programs offered by foundations, businesses, professional groups, and other organizations.

WHERE TO OBTAIN GOVERNMENT DOCUMENTS

The U.S. government seeks wide dissemination of government documents. Every geographic area has a *designated regional depository* of government documents that receives and retains one copy of each government publication in either printed or microfacsimile form. Distribution is made to libraries by the Office of the Superintendent of Documents. Publications are permanently retained even after they have ceased to be available from the Superintendent of Documents. Some libraries are designated as "restricted" depositories and are allowed to maintain publications of particular types. Every major metropolitan area has at least one primary regional depository and often has several other restricted depositories. A call to the nearest library is usually sufficient to discover where the regional depository is located. A listing of depository libraries can be ordered from Chief of the Library, Department of Public Documents, U.S. Government Printing Office, Washington, D.C. 20402. Many libraries that are not designated depositories receive some government publications as well.

In addition, the U.S. Government Printing Office publishes a catalog of documents, including list prices. Various types of documents are listed, from the statistical reports of the Census Bureau to information pamphlets on various topics. It is generally possible to obtain single copies of many of the shorter publications at no cost.

Although the government provides much information routinely, not all information is widely disseminated. Special studies and reports of agencies may not be released to the general public. Many of these documents are available upon request; however, such requests may need to be made under the Freedom of Information Act.

OBTAINING INFORMATION UNDER
THE FREEDOM OF INFORMATION ACT

There is nothing difficult about obtaining information under the Freedom of Information Act. You need only identify the information desired in a letter of request. It is not even necessary to state why you need the information. The law requires that an agency receiving a request under the act respond to requests in some manner within ten working days. However, this does not mean that the information will be sent quickly. The Freedom of Information Act is far from foolproof, and different agencies handle requests quite differently. Futhermore, the determination of what constitutes exempted information is largely left to the discretion of administrators. Ironically, in some agencies, documents that might otherwise be more readily available now require a formal request under the Freedom of Information Act.

Many agencies have specified officers who are responsible for information requests. To speed the processing of requests, it usually is wise to write ''Freedom of Information Request'' both on the top of the request and on the envelope in which it is mailed. The act allows agencies to charge for information, but these charges cannot exceed the actual cost of searching for and copying documents. As of 1983, search fees were computed at $5.00 per hour and copying costs were $.10 cents per page. If the charge is modest or the information was produced for general use, there may be no charge. There are also four circumstances under which you may avoid paying all or some of these charges: (1) if you are an indigent; (2) if the information would benefit the general public; (3) if in making a request you set a dollar limit or ceiling on costs; or (4) if you ask to examine the documents at the agency rather than purchasing them.

Information produced by Congress (or by congressional agencies such as the Library of Congress), the Government Printing Office, and the federal judicial system is not covered under the act. Presidential papers are also exempt. Even for agencies to which the act applies, the following nine categories of information are exempt from the act:

(1) Classified information on national defense and foreign policy. Government secrets and confidential material are also covered by this provision. Upon receipt of a request, agencies are required to review the information to determine if it should remain classified.

(2) Information exempt under other laws (such as income tax returns) or that is prohibited from release by law.

(3) Internal communications, such as intra-agency and interagency memoranda.

(4) Personal and private information such as medical records and personnel files, if release would constitute an invasion of privacy.

(5) Information from investigatory files, if release would interfere with law enforcement, be an invasion of privacy, expose confidential sources or investigative techniques, endanger a life, or deprive someone of the right to a fair trial.

(6) Information about financial institutions such as the Federal Reserve Board.

(7) Information about wells, including certain maps.

(8) Internal personnel practices and rules that do not involve interests of individuals outside of the agency.

(9) Confidential business information. Designed to exempt trade secrets and confidential financial data, this exemption has been the most controversial of the nine. The determination of what does or does not fall under this exemption is unclear and is left largely to the discretion of administrators.

If only a portion of the information requested falls under an exemption, the rest of the material must be released. If a request is denied, the agency involved must provide notification, the reasons for the denial, the names and addresses of those responsible for the denial, and information concerning the appeal process. The right of appeal is guaranteed by the act, although most agencies require that appeals be filed within 30 days of the notification of denial. Appeals are frequently successful. Furthermore, court action may be taken if the appeal is denied. More information about the Freedom of Information Act can be obtained from the Freedom of Information Clearing House, P.O. Box 19307, Washington, DC 20036.

One problem associated with obtaining information under the Freedom of Information Act is that of knowing what to ask for. You must be able to provide a "reasonable" description of the information you want. One approach to this problem is to examine request letters to agencies. These letters, which become a part of the public record, are often kept in reading rooms maintained by agencies. Examining requests provides a useful means for identifying what information may be available from a particular agency. A second problem with information requests is one of time. Requests may require several months to fill, depending on the nature and amount of the information sought and whether an appeal is necessary. Several useful publications related to the Freedom of Information Act are listed below:

• *The Freedom of Information Act: What It Is and How to Use It*
Order this from the Freedom of Information Clearinghouse. Single copies are free.

• *A Citizen's Guide on How to Use the Freedom of Information Act and the Privacy Act in Requesting Government Documents*
This volume was compiled by the House Committee on Government Operations. It can be ordered from the Government Printing Office.

• *The Federal Register Index*
This monthly index is bound into quarterly cumulative indexes. It lists what is available from each federal agency through the Freedom of Information Act, how much it costs, and where it can be purchased or examined. Unfortunately, not all government agencies submit such lists. The index can be ordered from the Government Printing Office.

SUMMARY

The list of information sources above is quite selective. It provides only an introduction to the variety of sources of data available from the government. A useful introduction to the use of government data for problem solving is *A Handbook for Business on the Use of Government Statistics* (May, 1979). Another useful reference is *Social Statistics in Use* (Hauser, 1975). This latter book describes how statistics are compiled, where they are available, and how they may be used by educators, planners, government, business, and the general public.

EXERCISES

Exercise 4.1: If you were involved in the financial services industry, how would you determine what percentage of individual gross incomes goes into savings? How would you determine whether this percentage was going up, down, or remaining the same?

Exercise 4.2: If you were involved in long-range planning for a school district, how would you determine whether adequate classroom space would be available in five years? In ten years?

Exercise 4.3: Select any topic. Determine what federal agencies provide support for research on this topic.

Exercise 4.4: Assume you are in the business of producing blivets. Blivets are sold to several government agencies, including the Department of Defense and the Department of the Interior. How would you identify opportunities to sell blivets to government agencies?

Exercise 4.5: Is the incidence of larceny increasing in the United States? What about murder?

5

Syndicated Commercial and Other Nongovernment Sources of Information

Information acquisition and analysis is a large commercial industry. Numerous firms routinely obtain and make available specialized information. Such information includes marketing research studies, trade association publications, customized research on particular topics, and econometric data. These data are generally sold to users, but they often lose their commercial value with time and can be obtained at a modest cost. This chapter introduces some of the more common types of syndicated information, discusses how to use these sources, and offers the advantages and disadvantages of using these sources.

Many private organizations also produce data, reports, and other forms of information. This information ranges from customized applications of data collected by government sources to the results of rather extensive primary data collection efforts. Many firms are in the information business, supplying data and reports on specialized topics to member organizations or client companies. Data from those sources are frequently not free; rather, individuals and organizations pay a fee to obtain the information. However, since much of this information may be collected simultaneously, the costs of data collection are often shared by all parties. Thus it may be significantly less expensive to use these data sources then to do one's own research.

Much of the proprietary information available in the United States is designed to aid business interests with specific needs. These needs range from tracking the sales of products to learning something about the media habits of people toward whom advertising will be directed. Because such information offers a competitive advantage to firms possessing it, access to the data is often restricted. However, it is not unusual for information to lose its competitive value with time and to become more freely available.

The cost and restricted availability of proprietary data and reports are not the only potential disadvantages of using this type of information. Data are generally collected with specific objectives in mind, and may not be useful for other purposes. Definitions of terms and categories may vary widely across sources, making comparisons difficult or even impossible. The reliability and consistency of data may also vary widely from source to source, necessitating careful scrutiny of the data and the procedures used to obtain it.

Despite these limitations, there are some important advantages to using data from these sources. It is almost always less expensive to obtain information from these sources than it is to do primary research. It is often possible to use data in ways for which they were not originally intended. Finally, because users are charged for the information, there is an incentive to ensure quality and consistency on the part of the information providers.

Two broad classes of proprietary data exist. The first is often referred to as *syndicated* data; the second is *customized* data. Whenever information may be useful to multiple users, the costs of obtaining information are high, and the information must be obtained and updated frequently, it is not uncommon for the users involved to pool resources to obtain the information. Trade associations often provide a vehicle for this type of resource pooling. Alternatively, a commercial firm may offer to provide such information to each user for a fee. Generally, with this type of service, the data collection and reporting procedures are standardized. The data are collected on a regular basis and then "syndicated" to various users. The well-known Nielsen Ratings of television audiences is an example of one such syndicated service.

As useful as syndicated services are, they often do not answer questions that a specific organization or individual may have. Thus it is often necessary to commission "customized" studies to meet specific information needs. Customized studies may also involve the pooling of resources, but the data are usually collected only once to answer a specific question or set of questions at a particular point in time. For example, a government agency may wish to determine the patterns of usage of its mass transit system. It may either conduct the study itself or commission a private organization to do it.

Many commercial firms provide both standardized (syndicated) and customized research services. Table 5.1 provides a listing of a number of the better-known organizations that do demographic research. Some of these firms merely reanalyze census bureau data; others offer to collect their own data. The list is not exhaustive, but it does provide a perspective on the types of data that may be obtained from commercial sources. A useful guide to customized studies is *FINDEX: The Directory of Market Research Reports, Studies, and Surveys,* published by the Information

(text continues on page 79)

TABLE 5.1
Directory of Demographic Data Firms

Allstate Research and Planning Center

Allstate is using the same program that it developed for the 1970 census to analyze 1980 occupational data and plan how companies can meet government equal employment guidelines. Starting with the census tract where the employer is located, the Allstate package traces the potential labor market for each occupation, depending on how far people in that occupation are willing to commute.

CACI

CACI sells demographic profiles of sites and trading areas, and disseminates demographic statistics through a number of computer time-sharing services. The firm plans to supply 1980 census data, as it did for the 1970 census. It is developing proprietary software for processing this data. It also offers other information derived from the census, including color mapping.

Chase Econometrics

Chase Econometrics specializes in economic forecasting. Its consumer market services makes quarterly forecasts (projecting 10 years into the future) of demographic characteristics such as household composition and income distribution by age. Subscribers receive regular reports analyzing consumer demand and spending in the light of Chase's economic and demographic predictions. Chase's databases and forecasting models can also be accessed directly. The recent acquisition of Regional Data Associates has expanded Chase's regional forecasting program, which now includes the states and over 100 metropolitian areas.

Claritas

Claritas provides demographic data for geographic regions defined by zip codes, school districts, congressional districts, retail trading areas, television markets, and so on. Its newest service is the PRIZM "cluster system" (discussed in Chapter 3). PRIZM classifies neighborhoods into some 40 types based on an analysis of the demographic characteristics of individual zip code areas. Clients can use this classification to project consumption patterns, target readership or media audiences, or organize direct-mail campaigns.

Compucon

Compucon provides computer-generated census tract maps. The firm is in the business of providing computer services to the telecommunications industry and originally developed the capability to do computer mapping for this industry. Customers can order maps for census tracts, cities, or SMSAs, including overlays of geographic landmarks or census data.

Compusearch

Compusearch offers both U.S. and Canadian demographic data from the 1976 Canadian Census, the 1980 U.S. Census, and current population and income estimates. Its computerized market research system is available via computer terminal or directly from the firm. Businesses can use the system to develop demographic profiles of customers, analyze market penetration, evaluate new sites, and target advertising.

(continued)

TABLE 5.1 Continued

Criterion

Criterion is a new firm that provides 1980 census data and current estimates of population and income in the form of computer-generated maps. Using transportation network analysis and the geographic data files of the Census Bureau, the firm also estimates travel-time contours to identify trading area boundaries. In addition, Criterion has a computer program that identifies and ranks market sites in metropolitan areas, blending information about the competitive environment with demographic information. Finally, Criterion has computer programs for human resources management and planning, and for evaluating company personnel data in light of census data for affirmative action reports.

Data Resources, Inc.

Data Resources, Inc. (DRI) is an econometrics firm that does a considerable amount of demographic research. For example, DRI's Demographic Economic Model (DECO) forecasts both population and income distributions to answer such questions as how the aging population affects consumption of durables and health expenditures. DRI has developed a new Consumer Allocation Model to look at expenditures by different demographic groups. This model can forecast how a particular price change, such as an increase in the cost of gas or a tax increase, for example, would affect the expenditures of, say, elderly single women. One way to use DRI is to subscribe to its Consumer Markets Service, a series of monthly bulletins that analyze and forecast consumer purchasing behavior. DRI also does customer market research.

Datamap

Datamap produces color-coded, computer-generated maps for use in trade area analysis and site location. The firm can combine census and other demographic data with data provided by the organization commissioning the research, such as information from sales slips or credit applications. These data are then plotted in quarter-mile or half-mile quadrants. In addition, Datamap can help clients — for instance, producers of consumer products, marketers, real estate firms, banks, and fast-food restaurants — to develop customer profiles for use in research.

Demographic Research Company

Demographic Research Company provides demographic data via the Rapidata time-sharing system or from the company. The firm provides such market research services as site evaluations, market rankings, targeted direct marketing, and computer graphics. In addition, its new economic analysis division has developed econometric models that can be used to forecast developments in the economy, and for particular industries or products. Demographic Research Company's clients include city and state planners as well as market researchers.

Distribution Sciences

Distribution Sciences is in the business of selling computerized transportation information. Its chief activity is to develop routing services for large corporations by analyzing freight bills. To facilitate its research, it has matched its database of place names to geographic codes and coordinates. Distribution Sciences also offers a computer tape containing the information necessary for matching zip coded regions to census data for states, counties, and other regions. The tape is updated twice a year.

TABLE 5.1 Continued

Donnelley Marketing

Donnelley Marketing, a Dun & Bradstreet subsidiary, sells demographic studies based on information from its direct-mail business combined with data from the census and other public sources. Its ZIProfile gives current demographic characteristics for each of the more than 37,000 zip code regions. Its Census Update provides current population, household, and income estimates for all census tracts. Both types of report are available on computer tape or in printed form. Donnelley Marketing plans to offer the entire spectrum of demographic data services. New products include complete 1980 census data through computer time sharing or call in, as well as geocoding.

DUALabs

DUALabs offers several services. The firm will select data from 1980 census tapes and put it on tape more efficiently than the Census Bureau. DUALabs guarantees purchasers of a score or more reels a net saving of at least $1000. DUALabs also offers online access to 1980 census data, as well as a 1980 Census Errata Activity Report Service ('80 EARS), which informs subscribers of errors in documentation, data, geographic coding, and so on, as they are discovered. The firm also offers computer programs for processing the 1980 census summary tapes. Because DUALabs is a nonprofit organization, its services are available only to members. Organizations that want tapes can join the File Reduction Consortium (for a one-time membership fee of $6000); organizations that want to use the online services can join the Public Data Network ($100 initiation fee, plus $100 per year, with additional fees for use of each service).

Financial Marketing Group, Inc.

This firm creates household information systems for retailers by merging sales account data with census data. Working primarily in the Mid-Atlantic area, the firm geocodes its clients' addresses and matches them to census data at the census tract level. Clients can buy the system outright, including the analytical software, or have the firm maintain it for them.

Geographic Data Technology

Geographic Data Technology maintains a nationwide digital map base used to provide geographic data services. A major service is specialized address matching and geocoding down to the block level and to geographic coordinates. The firm also designs more efficient distribution routes based on where a client's customers are located. It also develops more efficient political districts by interpreting such demographic characteristics as races of pupils in various school districts and voting patterns in electoral districts.

Geographic Systems

Geographic Systems analyzes demographic data and produces site evaluations and market analyses in both report and computer map form. One can purchase the firm's data base, computer programs, and geographic boundary files either in whole or in part. It also offers analysis and mapping for geographic areas, including zip code regions, down to the census tract. Its census tract boundary file includes centroids as well as area in square miles.

(continued)

TABLE 5.1 Continued

Infomap

Infomap creates computer maps combining census data and the client's own data for census tracts, counties, states, or regions. The firm has produced an *Atlas of Demographics: U.S. by County*, which contains a series of U.S. maps showing counties color coded according to sixteen demographic and socioeconomic characteristics.

International Data and Development

International Data and Development (IDD) offers population, income, and other demographic estimates, updated biennially, for census tracts and minor civil divisions. IDD also sells a range of computer programs designed for processing large databases, particularly the census. The company's Mod Series was the major processing software for the 1970 census, and IDD is updating it to accommodate the 1980 census format. In addition, IDD will use the 1980 census tapes to perform special tabulations or geographic analyses for clients.

Kellex Data

Kellex produces printed reports or computer tapes showing the demographics of people in particular occupations in any geographic area for affirmative action research.

Market Statistics

Market Statistics offers marketing and advertising analyses using demographic data. During the 1970s, the firm had access only to census data aggregated at the county level. However, in the 1980s, the firm will be developing the capability to aggregate data at the level of census tracts and zipcode regions. They plan to sell this service to local broadcasting and print media industries, who use this type of data extensively. In addition to consulting, Market Statistics provides census information through a system it calls CENTAB. This system lets clients specify a variety of demographic units ranging from a census tract to the total United States.

Metromail

Metromail provides demographic statistics for small areas based on its mailing lists. It also has a product called the Index of Social Position, which combines data on income and other related characteristics into a number that more accurately characterizes the social status of a neighborhood.

Modeling Systems

Modeling Systems applies mathematical models to transportation problems. Using the Census DIME file to determine block dimensions, the firm divides geographic areas into sections of any shapes and sizes, depending on what is required. Once the divisions have been established, other data can be added to census information to forecast demand.

National Decision Systems

National Decision Systems specializes in computer-produced reports that link demographic and geographic information in a variety of ways. Its clients can order site evaluations and consumer expenditure reports for areas within a one-, two-, or five-mile radius of a speci-

TABLE 5.1 Continued

fied site. Or they can use Site Search if they want to limit their site evaluation to populations with the demographic characteristics of product consumers. Site Search is done on a customized basis. Another product, Market Scan, uses the same procedure, but is a standard product based on the twenty most frequently requested demographic characteristics for metropolitan areas.

National Planning Data Corporation

National Planning Data Corporation provides both standard and customized census data services. Its small-area population and income statistics from the census are updated annually. The firm supplements these annual estimates with five-year population and household statistical projections. Both services cover the entire country, and both are used primarily by businesses for consumer marketing purposes. The company is planning to offer computer graphics and mapping services, and may also integrate data from other Census Bureau surveys such as the Current Population Survey, County Business Patterns, and the economic censuses.

Orrington Economics, Inc.

Orrington Economics provides data products for microcomputers. It offers a database of 40 demographic and retail trade statistics for all states, and retail trade statistics for all states and 38 SMSAs on a computer diskette that can be used on Apple II, TRS 80, and IBM personal computers. Their information is based on census data. This database can be analyzed using VISICALC software.

Personnel Research, Inc.

PRI provides statistical analyses for Equal Employment Opportunity (EEO) litigation and for affirmative action planning by relating census and other public data to clients' personnel files. The firm designs affirmative action plans that can be customized to fit the client's needs. PRI also sells data from the Census/EEO Special File in booklets or on computer tape by state, county, and SMSA.

Public Demographics, Inc.

This company was established in 1981 to apply demographic analysis to solving community problems. Its first product, STATUS-1, displays demographic statistics for any geographical area on a color computer map. A new product, MARKITS, analyzes the economic potential of a given community or commercial district by displaying the area's demographics (using UDS's COLORSITE program) and its buying and behavior patterns (using Claritas's PRIZM).

R. L. Polk and Co.

R. L. Polk provides demographic data for neighborhoods in those cities where it produces annual city directories. Based on door-to-door canvassing, Polk's Profiles of Change service describes both current status and recent changes in the demographic characteristics of neighborhoods. Reports include both maps and test. Local government agencies have been Polk's main clients, but the firm is also planning to sell Profiles of Change to the private sector. Insurance companies, real estate developers, newspapers, retailers, banks, and savings and loans institutions will be able to order Polk's neighborhood-based annual income estimates.

(continued)

TABLE 5.1 Continued

Robinson Associates

Robinson Associates combines census information, research available from other sources, company data, and field research, and develops a marketing strategy for clients. Using mathematical techniques, the firm constructs computer models of a given marketplace.

Sammamish Data Systems

This firm sells microcomputer diskettes of 1980 census data. In addition, data from summary tape files are available on diskettes for states or portions of states.

Survey Sampling

Survey Sampling's primary business is to create telephone samples for surveying households or business firms. The firm uses 1980 census data, including the zip code tabulation, to develop customer profiles for every telephone exchange nationwide as well as for standard geographic areas. Survey Sampling recently completed keypunching all Yellow Page directories, which enables it to distinguish business telephone numbers from consumer numbers.

Urban Data Processing

Urban Data Processing is known for doing address matching, which involves coding address lists by census tract so that the holders of address lists can analyze them for demographic characteristics. The company also offers site selection and market analysis systems. Both systems blend census statistics with a client's proprietary information. Although the firm's principal clients are in the banking, insurance, and retail industries, its services can be used by any organization that has a name and address file.

Urban Decision Systems

Urban Decision System (UDS) offers census data in a variety of forms, depending on the needs of its clients. Those who can program a computer in FORTRAN and have a computer terminal available can build census data files to their own specifications using UDS's CENSAC (census access) system. Other UDS systems include ONSITE, which produces standard site evaluation and trade area reports; TELE/SITE, which lets people who do not have a computer terminal order the ONSITE reports by telephone; and Market Base, which provides demographic statistics for zip code regions, counties, SMSAs, and so forth. UDS has designed two new systems to go with the 1980 census data: SCAN/U.S. searches a given geographic region to identify areas with high incidences of a particular demographic characteristic. Another new product, COLORSITE, reports demographic data on colored maps and charts, either on slides or on paper.

Urban Science Applications, Inc.

Urban Science Applications uses computer graphics and mapping to select optimal locations for automobile dealerships, banks, and shopping centers. The firm combines its clients' own data with census data at the tract level to produce customized reports. Alternatively, clients may lease the hardware and software and do their own analyses, drawing on the firm's expertise for help when needed.

TABLE 5.1 Continued

Vistar, Inc.

This firm provides OCTAGON, a software package for microcomputers similar to the Census Bureau's CENSPAC for mainframe computers. The package can be used by any microcomputer using a CP/M operating system. OCTAGON has several programs for analyzing demographic data supplied by either Vistar or the user. Vistar was established in 1978, and until now has worked primarily in the real estate industry supplying small area housing data for analysis by OCTAGON. One of Vistar's new products is EVE, an English-language query system for microcomputers that allows the user to ask, for example, "How many people under 29 years old live in D census tract?" and receive an answer in English.

Warren Glimpse and Co.

Warren Glimpse specializes in extracting and cross-tabulating data from census summary and microdata tapes. The firm also offers workshops for people interested in learning how to use census data files.

Wharton EFA, Inc.

Wharton builds economic and demographic forecasting models for SMSAs, counties, and states based on its national economic model. The models then belong to its clients, who can use them in conjunction with the firm's time-sharing system, database, econometric model, and software. Wharton brings the model up to date annually, and offers customized forecasts for specific demographic groups.

SOURCE: Adapted from Riche (1983). Copyright 1983 by American Demographics, Inc. Used by permission.

Clearinghouse. *FINDEX* is published annually, with midyear supplements. It lists published, commercially available market and business research reports. The most recent edition includes over 5000 reports from more than 300 research publishers. Although designed primarily as an aid to business researchers, the reports are often useful to others as well. Information on such varied topics as health care, transportation, energy, computers and electronics, media, travel and tourism, and basic industries such as petrochemicals and metals are listed. The name of the organization offering the information is provided, along with an estimated cost of the report. The price of a report may be as much as several thousand dollars; however, many of the publications are available at modest cost.

The international analogue of *FINDEX* is the *International Directory of Published Market Research*, compiled by the British Overseas Trade Board (1979) in collaboration with Arlington Management Publications. This directory lists over 5000 studies from over 100 nations.

Many corporations provide information on a variety of topics. These range from reports to stockholders to descriptions of how products are manufactured and used. For example, Hershey Foods publishes a number of brochures on chocolate that contain information on nutrition, recipes, and related topics. A useful guide to these publications is *Corporate Publications in Print* (Norback, 1980).

Trade associations are also an invaluable source of information. Almost every industry, from grape growing to banking, has one or more trade associations. These associations often sponsor studies that they make available to members and, often, to outsiders as well. They may also publish or sponsor publication of specialized reports. A significant amount of very detailed information is often available in trade publications. Table 5.2 illustrates the number of publications available regarding just one industry, the beverage industry. There are several useful guides to trade associations. Among these are the *National Trade and Professional Associations of the United States* (Colgate and Fowler, 1983), the *Encyclopedia of Associations, Trade Directories of the World*, and the *Directory of European Associations* (1976). Many directories are also compiled for specific industries. Two very useful guides to such directories are the *Guide to American Directories* (1978), which lists over 6000 trade, professional, and industrial directories, and *Guide to American Scientific and Technical Directories* (1975).

The number of firms providing syndicated or customized research is far too large to allow a summary of all of them in this chapter. There are, however, several common objectives for commissioning research. Therefore, the remainder of this chapter discusses the most frequent uses of this information by administrators and businesses. This is not to suggest that there are no other uses of the data. Indeed, such additional uses will be pointed out as appropriate.

GENERAL INFORMATION ABOUT COMPANIES

A common information requirement of many organizations is information about other organizations. There are a number of very useful guides to commercial organizations in the United States and abroad; several of the better known are listed in Table 5.3. Most of these guides are quite general, but describe how to obtain access to additional information. SIC codes (the Standard Industrial Classifications used by the Census Bureau) are particularly useful, since many other sources list information by SIC code. The identification of the manufacturer(s) of particular products or brands is also extremely helpful. For example, if one needs to research personal computers, these guides will provide a basis for identifying the firms that manufacture them and the associated SIC codes. This information is then the basis for further data collection efforts.

TABLE 5.2
Selected Trade Publications Relevant to the
Beverage Industry

Publication	Content
Beer Marketer's Insights	broad discussion of current developments in the brewing industry
Beverage Industry	detailed reporting of developments in key beverage areas, especially soft drinks
Beverage World	in-depth coverage of leading beverage areas
Brewers Almanac	beer industry statistics
Business Week	annual studies on liquor and tobacco industries
DISCUSS Fact Book	discussion of the alcoholic beverage industry's place in society
IMPACT	beer, wine, and spirits data and articles
LNA Ad $ Summary	advertising expenditures totaled by brand
The Liquor Handbook	wide-ranging compilation of industry statistics
Modern Brewery Age	timely discussion of beer industry
NSDA Sales Survey	national and regional industry statistics
Sugar and Sweetener Report	thorough market report
The Wine Marketing Handbook	wide-ranging compilation of industry statistics
Wines & Vines	articles and statistics on the wine industry

TABLE 5.3
Sources of Information About Commercial Organizations

Directory of American Firms Operating in Foreign Countries
Lists over 4500 American companies and countries of operation.

Dun & Bradstreet Million Dollar Directory
Volume 1 lists some 47,000 U.S. companies worth $1 million or more. Volume 2 lists over 31,000 U.S. companies valued at $500,000 to $999,999. Information on products, officers, sales, number of employees, and SIC codes is provided.

Dun & Bradstreet Principal International Businesses
A guide to some 51,000 leading companies in 135 countries.

EIS Plants and EIS Establishments
EIS Plants provides data on the approximately 130,000 industrial companies with 20 or more employees. In contrast, *EIS Establishments* includes data on some 200,000 nonmanufacturing organizations. The information provided includes location of headquarters, major branches, share of the market, number of employees, and estimated sales volume.

F&S Index to Corporations and Industries, United States (published by Predicasts, Inc.)
This publication provides information on over 750 business and financial publications. It is probably the best single index for finding current informaton on U.S. companies and industries. Published weekly, with monthly, quarterly, and annual cummulations, it is indexed by company and SIC code.

F&S Index, Europe and F&S Index, International
These are both companion volumes to *F&S Index, United States.* They are published monthly, with quarterly and annual cummulations. Both volumes are indexed by SIC code, region and country, and company.

Kelly's Manufacturers and Merchants Directory
A world directory with special emphasis on the British Isles.

Marketing Economics: Key Plants
A listing of plants with 100 or more employees, indexed by state, country, and SIC code.

Sheldon's Retail Directory of the United States and Canada
An annual guide to the largest chain and independent retail operations in these two countries.

Standard & Poor's Register of Corporations, Directors, and Executives
A three-volume guide to over 37,000 U.S. and Canadian corporations. Volume 1 provides an alphabetical listing of corporations, their products, officers, SIC codes, number of employees, and sales figures. Volume 2 provides information on executives and directors of the corporation. Volume 3 contains economic indices by SIC code and geographical region.

TABLE 5.3 Continued

Thomas Register of American Manufacturers
This publication is a comprehensive guide to American manufacturing. Firms are indexed by company name, product(s) produced, and brand names.

Who Owns Whom (North American edition)
A guide to U.S. and Canadian parent companies, subsidiaries, and associate companies. Volumes are also available for Australia, the Far East, Continental Europe, the United Kingdom, and Ireland.

FINANCIAL DATA ON ORGANIZATIONS

Rather detailed financial information is available about many organizations. Not only are 10-Ks (the detailed reports filed by corporations, discussed in Chapter 4) available from the SEC, but numerous firms also provide highly specialized information relevant to financial performance in the industry. This information may range from general overviews of the financial performances and activities of a variety of industries to details related to a specific industry. Such information is often used by potential investors, by firms engaged in analyses of competitors, and by researchers in economics, finance, and accounting. The number of publications dealing with financial aspects of organizations is far too large for a comprehensive listing in this chapter. Table 5.4 describes some of the more frequently used publications. The reference librarians of most libraries can provide information about other sources.

MARKETING AND CONSUMER INFORMATION

A wealth of data are available on how people spend their time and money. Such information is particularly valuable to firms engaged in selling products and services, but is also useful to economists, anthropologists, sociologists, and social psychologists who are interested in the socioeconomic characteristics of a society and its culture. The largest syndicated research services provide information on the public's buying and media habits, lifestyles, and attitudes and opinions. The potential for using such services for research purposes is well illustrated by one firm, Behavior Scan.

The Behavior Scan system collects information about supermarket purchases (as captured with optical scanners), manipulates television commercials shown in individual homes via cable, and conducts comprehensive surveys (Eskin, 1981). Participating in this research system are 2000 households in 2 different geographic areas. Each household

TABLE 5.4
Sources of Information on Finance Records

Barron's Market Laboratory (Farrell, annual)

An annual compilation of stock market statistics for the previous year.

Corporate Profiles for Executives and Investors

Provides data on over 2000 major U.S. corporations, including a five-year review of sales, earnings and dividends, and a two-year review of assets and debts. Published annually.

Corporation Records

Provides the latest financial statistics on companies, with background information and news related to the organization's operations.

Dow Jones Investor's Handbook

Published annually by Dow Jones and Company, this publication gives daily Dow Jones averages for the current year, monthly closing averages, dividend yield, and price-earnings for over ten years. *The Dow Jones Averages, 1885-1970* provides useful historical statistics.

Dun's Financial Profiles

Provides customized reports based on a financial database of over 800,000 private and public businesses. For a fee, Dun & Bradstreet will produce a report of financial ratios, with historical and industry norms, for aggregates of businesses based on SIC code, geographical region, and number of employees, whether public or private or some combination of these items.

Fortune Double 500 Directory

Provides information on the 1000 largest U.S. corporations, 50 largest banks, and 50 largest life insurance, financial, transportation, utility, and retailing companies, including assets, profits and sales. Appears in the May-August issues of *Fortune* each year.

Moody's Manuals

Moody's publishes seven manuals each year and provides weekly updates. The manuals include *Banks and Finance* (including insurance, real estate, and investment companies), *Transportation, OTC* (over-the-counter) *Industrial, Municipal and Government, Public Utility,* and *International.* Information provided includes current and historical financial data, securities information, location of the company, a brief history of the company, and the officers of the organization.

Standard & Poor's Stock Reports

Three separate publications are available, one on the New York Stock Exchange, one on the American Exchange, and one on over-the-counter and regional exchanges. Each report provides brief descriptions of companies, earnings and balance sheet data, capitalizations, and so on.

Value Line Investment Survey

A four-volume publication that provides ratings and reports on approximately 1700 stocks.

has an identification card that is presented when purchases are made at the supermarket. This card provides a means for identifying all of the purchases, on an item-by-item basis, made by the household. This information can then be related to consumer attitudes or to differences in promotional activities directed at these households. For example, the effect of a particular type of advertising may be evaluated by selectively exposing some of the households to commercials. Scanner data may then be employed to evaluate the effect of the advertising on purchasing behavior. This service provides an opportunity for experiments in a relatively natural environment. Although the service is not inexpensive, it is a practical and cost-effective means for many organizations to collect information on their marketing programs. Such information would otherwise be impractical or too costly for a single firm to acquire. Behavior Scan also provides certain types of data to academic researchers at a nominal charge.

There are numerous other sources of information about people and organizations. One of the most common sources of such information is the mail panel. Mail panels are composed of households that have agreed to participate in periodic mail surveys. These surveys may ask for attitudes and opinions on political events, plans for purchases in the future, reactions to products or services, or time spent in various activities. Because members of mail panels are generally very cooperative and the costs of collecting the data are shared by many users, mail panels are a relatively inexpensive means of obtaining a great deal of information. In 1979, at least seven syndicated panels were available in the United States and Canada and still others were available in other parts of the world (Sudman & Ferber, 1979). Perhaps the best known of these is the Nielson television viewing panel. Some universities and not-for-profit organizations also operate mail panels. For example, the University of Arkansas operates a panel that is generally characteristic of the population of the state of Arkansas.

A variation of the mail panel is the mail-diary panel. Members of these panels maintain diaries of various activities. Market Research Corporation of American (MRCA) is among the oldest mail-diary panel operations. Approximately 7500 families throughout the United States provide the MRCA with detailed descriptions of their purchase habits by keeping diaries. They record such information as what was purchased, when and where the purchase was made, how much it cost, the quantity purchased, the number of items in the package, and whether the purchase involved a special deal. Each month MRCA provides a report of consumer purchases during the previous month, by product category and brand. The families participating in the diary panel are selected to be representative of the larger population with respect to such characteristics as geography, income, presence of children, family size, age, and education. They are not necessarily representative with respect to other characteristics, however, so some caution must be excercised with respect to broad generalizations about very specific behaviors.

Arbitron is another vendor of diary-panels. Its principal concerns are the television viewing and radio listening habits of individuals. People recruited for the Arbitron panel keep diaries of their media habits, and this information is compiled and reported each month. These data also provide the basis for special reports on topics such as changing media habits and media habits of selected subpopulations.

ADVANTAGES AND DISADVANTAGES OF MAIL PANELS

Mail panels are a cost-effective means for obtaining a great deal of information. Since data are collected continuously, it is possible to track changes over time and thus to conduct quasi-experiments.

Despite these advantages, there are also drawbacks. Panel members are volunteers. Selection bias may well be present in these panels, since as few as one in five households contacted agree to serve on such panels. Also, people drop out of panels, move, or die. The result is that panel membership changes over time. From year to year, panel member turnover may range from 20 percent to 33 percent. Therefore, differences over time may reflect only the mortality rate of the sample. There is little control over who completes the questionnaires. Thus information that might best be obtained from a particular member of the household might be distorted or missed altogether because someone else in the household completed the questionnaire. Members of mail panels are subject to a variety of testing effects. New members often develop a "social consciousness" that distorts behavior and reports of behavior. Long-time members often become habituated to questionnaires, new products, and so on. Finally, these panels may not be fully representative of the larger population with respect to behavior, opinions, and other characteristics of interest. While efforts are made to correct these problems by not using data of new panel members for a period after recruitment and by rotating old members off the panel, they still represent potential sources of bias. Nevertheless, such panels provide useful insights into the attitudes and behavior of individuals.

Special-purpose panels are often available. For example, panels of single persons, physicians, and engineers are available. Obviously, the most relevant and immediate use of panel data is by major corporations that are trying to understand their customers. Many firms will provide access to panel data for social science researchers, however.

In addition to continuous panels, a number of organizations survey the population (or a subset of the population) using systematic sampling. The Survey Research Institute of the University of Michigan conducts a number of ongoing surveys dealing with significant social issues. Data from, and reports of, these surveys are available to researchers. One of the largest surveys of households is carried out by a commercial research firm, Mediamark Research Inc. (MRI; formerly called Target Group Index, or TGI). Approximately 30,000 households are involved in the interviewing process. The sample is a strict probability sample of the adult population of the continental United States. Cluster sampling is used to identify households for participation in the study. The primary purpose of the MRI survey is to gather information on magazine audiences for use by advertisers. The survey obtains demographic information, magazine and newspaper readership, product usage, other selected activities, and some data on television and radio audiences. These data are then summarized in a series of volumes that are arranged by magazine readership and product category.

MRI is a convenient source of information about the characteristics of people who engage in certain activities, such as purchasing particular products or stocks, or participating in sports or civic activities. Most advertising agencies have current copies of MRI, and many business school libraries maintain back issues. These back issues provide a useful means for examining trends in behavior over time. The Simmons organization provides similar data and reports.

There are numerous other sources of secondary data that compute information about the behavior of individuals and organizations. These range from opinion polling organizations to firms that monitor the sales of goods and services. A useful guide to these firms is the *International Directory of Marketing Research Houses and Services*, published annually by the New York Chapter of the American Marketing Association. This publication lists marketing research firms in the United States and selected foreign countries and describes the services provided by these firms. Also helpful is *Bradford's Directory of Marketing Research Agencies and Management Consultants in the U.S. and the World*. This directory also provides a description of the services offered by various research firms. Table 5.5 describes several services and illustrates that a variety of services are available. Some of these firms make sample reports and other materials available upon request.

INFORMATION ON FOREIGN COUNTRIES

Another frequent area of interest for both businesses and academic researchers is the foreign arena. Much information is available from for-

TABLE 5.5
Commercial Research Services Offering
Syndicated and Customized Reports

A.C. Nielson Co.
Nielson offers a wide range of services, from the television rating service to media diary panels to store audits. Store audits provide information on sales by retail units. Other data obtained in these audits include prices, displays, shelf facings, and various other characteristics of retail units.

Audits and Surveys
This company conducts an annual census of retail product distribution for infrequently purchased products. In addition, it carries out bimonthly store audits of more frequently purchased products.

Belden Associates
Provides ongoing studies related to newspaper readership.

Broadcasting Publications, Inc.
Publishes a directory of U.S. and Canadian radio and television stations, including cable stations.

Burke Marketing Research
Provides a variety of marketing research services.

Gallup Organization, Inc.
The grandfather of opinion polling organizations, Gallup conducts an omnibus national survey every two to four weeks. Every month, it publishes a newsletter for business executives assessing public attitudes. It also produces numerous special topic reports.

Louis Harris and Associates, Inc.
Publishes numerous reports of special-purpose opinion surveys.

Merchandising
Merchandising is a monthly publication. It provides numerous special reports. Its "Statistical and Marketing Report" presents data on the sales, replacement, trade-in, and product saturation of major electronics products and appliances. Its annual "Consumers Survey" provides information on consumer discretionary spending, attidues toward warranties, product information search, and so on.

Opinion Research Corporation (ORC)
ORC Public Opinion Index tracks opinions of the general public, executives, government leaders, the media, and the financial community. It offers numerous reports of special surveys and several special-purpose syndicated services.

TABLE 5.5 Continued

Predicasts
Tracks economic indicators, industries, and products. Provides forecasts for various industry groups and product categories.

Roper Organization
Publishes "Roper Reports" and "Roper Reports Index," which are based on data collected via personal interviews.

Sales and Marketing Management
A serial providing annual special issues that are useful for analyzing markets. The "Survey of Buying Power" issues in July and October of each year provide data on population, retail sales, and effective buying income for U.S. and Canadian markets. An annual "Survey of Industrial Purchasing Power" (in April) and "Survey of Selling Costs" (in February) are also published.

Selling Areas-Marketing, Inc. (SAMI)
A sales tracking service offered to organizations. Reports are based on the movement of goods from warehouses to the retail level. A supplement to SAMI is the SAMI Retail Distribution Index (SARDI), which provides data on product movement out of retail outlets.

World Advertising Expenditures
This annual volume provides estimates of advertising expenditures in various media categories by country.

Yankelovich, Skelly, and White
Publishes "Services Offered by the Firm," which describes the full range of services offered by the organization. The "Yankelovich Monitor" reports the results of a survey that tracks 35 social trends in the general population.

---

eign governments, the U.S. government, and the United Nations. In addition, there is also a substantial amount of information available from commercial sources. Several sources of such information that are particularly useful are the following: *Statesman's Yearbook* provides brief facts about government, population, education, finance, industries, and the like for each country of the world. *Worldcasts*, published by Predicasts, Inc., provides short-term and long-term forecasts of economic indicators for specific countries. Price Waterhouse and Company publishes a series of *Doing Business in . . .* books that provide basic historical, economic, and social data on many countries, as well as other facts relevant to conducting business in these countries. *BI-DATA: Printout Summary*, published by Business International Corporation, is a compendium of information on 70 nations. The December issues of the weekly *Business International* provide similar data for 132 countries. *Pick's Currency Yearbook* is a useful guide to 112 foreign currencies. Finally, the *Encyclopedia of Geographic Information Sources* (Wasserman et al., 1978) describes sources of information on foreign nations.

SUMMARY

Commercial sources of information are an invaluable resource. The data provided generally address rather specific issues and problems. However, since many firms provide this information at a profit, it is sometimes costly relative to government sources. There may also be restrictions on availability. Despite these limitations, the data are generally less costly than would be the case if they were collected directly by the user. Also, as information ages, it often loses its commercial value and becomes more readily accessible. This latter fact is largely unknown to many social scientists, who neglect to seek out commercially available data. Such data are often the least expensive and most reliable means for tracking changes in the social structure and culture of our nation.

EXERCISES

Exercise 5.1: What can you learn from commercially available sources about the characteristics of the frequent leisure traveler? Develop a profile of this traveler.

Exercise 5.2: What trade associations might provide information about the dietary habits of American adolescents? Are there any trade journals that would provide information on this topic?

Exercise 5.3: Write several of the public opinion polling organizations for a description of their services. Critique their data collection procedures.

Exercise 5.4: Using whatever secondary sources you can identify, answer the following question: Are Americans replacing a work ethic with a leisure ethic?

Exercise 5.5: Using whatever secondary sources you can identify, answer the following question: Are Americans more concerned about nutrition today than 10 years ago?

Exercise 5.6: What sources of information would you examine when doing a financial analysis of a corporation?

6

Computer-Assisted
Information Acquisition

Much information has been transferred to or indexed on computer systems. These computer systems provide rapid and efficient access to a tremendous volume of information. Exhaustive information searches can often be completed within a few minutes by using these systems. This chapter discusses the use of these systems.

The advent of the computer age has created a revolution in information technology. The slow, methodical search through catalogs, directories, guides, and reference volumes is rapidly being replaced by the quick, thorough, and efficient computer search. Instead of spending months digging through libraries to locate information, one needs only a few minutes of computer time. An entire industry of online computer information services has developed within the last decade. This industry and its technologies are advancing so rapidly that new developments occur weekly. Unfortunately, many users of information have not recognized that libraries, business firms, and government offices already have the capability to identify an enormous amount of information within a few minutes.

The principle behind the use of the computer for information searches is quite simple. One stores information in the computer and references it by key identifiers. For example, it is possible to store the information in the volumes of *Psychological Abstracts* on computer, referenced by key words from the title of each abstract, authors' names, and so on. To request information about a particular subject, one would simply enter relevant key words or names into the computer. The computer then identifies all abstracts related to the topic. For instance, a request for information about learning would produce a listing of all abstracts with the word "learning" in the title (probably several thousand titles).

The key to a successful computer search is the identification of the relevant key words and databases. Obviously, a word appearing frequently in papers, such as "learning," will produce an overwhelming list of references, many of which are not actually relevant to the topic of interest. Recognition of this problem has produced computer software that allows the searcher to combine terms, eliminate unwanted categories of information, and carry out hierarchical searches. Boolean logic (a logic derived

A "AND" B
(only elements in both
A and B are of interest)

A "OR" B
(elements in either
A or B of interest)

A "NOT" B
(Only elements of A which
are not included in B are
of interest)

Figure 6.1: Boolean Operators

from set theory that is used for computing combinations) is used to accomplish this end. Figure 6.1 illustrates the Boolean operations. For example, two or more key words might be combined using an "AND" statement. When two key words are linked by an AND, both words must appear for the reference to be identified. Going back to the prior example with learning, the searcher might quickly narrow down the number of citations found by combining the key term "learning" with the organism of primary interest, say, "gerbils." The specification "learning AND gerbils" identifies only those citations referenced by both key words.

Two other operations used to define the scope of a computer-assisted information search are "OR" and "NOT." The OR statement identifies a citation if it is referenced by either one of the key words. For example, "learning OR conditioning" will identify all citations in which either the term "learning" or the term "conditioning" occurs. The NOT operator ensures that citations referenced by certain key words will not be included, regardless of whether other relevant key words also appear. For example, "learning NOT human" would exclude citations involving human learning; "learning OR conditioning NOT human" would produce references to learning and conditioning studies not in human populations. The NOT operator must be used very carefully, because use can dramatically restrict the number of citations identified by a search.

Many computer-assisted searches can be carried out interactively. Thus the searcher may begin with a broad category and a large number of key words and gradually narrow the search as needed. Most search algorithms provide an indication of the number of citations found and allow the examination of the first few citations. If a very large number of citations is produced and many appear inappropriate, further restrictions via AND and NOT commands and by reducing the set of descriptors employed may reduce the volume of output. This hierarchial search procedure may be continued until only those citations desired remain. It may also happen that the citations produced are not at all what is desired. If a search is unsuccessful, it is likely that different key words must be used.

Key words are identified differently depending on the database. For some databases, only words appearing in the title are used to reference citations. For other databases, key words are selected from both the titles and abstracts of citations. One database, called LEXIS, which is used for examining legal issues, actually does word-by-word searches of all citations. Some understanding of a particular database is necessary to ensure that appropriate citations will be identified by the key words one plans to use. Generally, the actual search is done by the librarian, although in the future it is likely the general public will be able to conduct interactive searches of databases. Even though a librarian may carry out the actual search, it is very important that the searcher work closely with that individual to verify that a representative search is completed.

Even with the power of the computer, citations may be missed. This may occur because the literature is not in the database; it may predate the database, for example. Most databases do not contain citations prior to 1970. Another problem is that the citation may be in a source that is not included within the database. Or key words may not be appropriate for identifying important sources. Thus it is helpful to do some verification of the results of a computer-assisted search. For instance, one should check that well-known citations related to the area of interest are being picked up in the search. If not, a revision of key words may be necessary. Similarly, since most databases also allow searches by author, one can double check by also doing an author search using a well-known name in the field and seeing if the topic search also picked up these references.

TYPES OF DATABASES

There are many different types of databases from many different sources. Some are offered by the government, some by professional societies, and some by commercial firms. Some provide raw data, others provide abstracts of published work, and still others provide complete documents. A guide to computer databases may be found in the *Datapro Directory of Online Services*. This directory lists the nature of the service,

(text continues on page 100)

TABLE 6.1
Selected Online Data Sources

ABI/INFORM (Abstracted Business Information)
1971-present, updated monthly

Covers 550 international business management publications in such fields as economics, accounting, marketing, management science, insurance, and real estate.

ACCOUNTANTS
1974-present, updated quarterly

Provides coverage of international literature related to accounting.

AGRICOLA

Developed by the National Agricultural Library, this source references worldwide literature on agriculture and related topics. The Food and Nutrition section contains abstracts. This source represents the actual holdings of the National Agricultural Library.

AIM/ARM (Vocational and Technical Education)

A specialized index of information about vocational and technical education and related areas. It covers materials published between 1967 and 1976. More recent publications have been incorporated into ERIC (see below).

ALCOHOL USE/ABUSE
1968-present

References publications on alcoholism. Compiled by the Hazerden Foundation.

AMERICA: HISTORY AND LIFE
1964-present

Covers the full range of United States and Canadian history, area studies, and current affairs.

AMERICAN STATISTICS INDEX
1973-present, updated monthly

An index of the statistical publications of the U.S. government, with citations to the publications of over 400 federal agencies.

ADVERTISING AND MARKETING INTELLIGENCE (AMI)
1979-present, updated daily

Includes over 110,000 abstracts of articles selected from more than 60 trade and professional publications. Provides data on advertising campaigns, market research, consumer trends, consumer products, and government regulations.

BIOSIS PREVIEWS
1970-present, updated semimonthly

Provides access to over 3.7 million citations from BIOLOGICAL ABSTRACTS and BIOLOGICAL ABSTRACTS/RRM.

TABLE 6.1 Continued

BOOKS INFO

Contains citations of books currently in print. Provides information about author, title, publisher code, price, subject descriptors, LC card number, and ISBN number.

CA SEARCH (Chemistry)
1967-present

CHEMICAL ABSTRACTS SERVICE

Provides access to 5,900,000 key word phrases, bibliographic information, and index entries.

CHILD ABUSE AND NEGLECT
1965-present, updated semiannually

Produced by the National Center on Child Abuse and Neglect.

COMPREHENSIVE DISSERTATION INDEX
1861-present, updated monthly

Includes most dissertations in the United States and selected foreign dissertations. Citations are provided so that abstracts may be found in the published *Comprehensive Dissertation Index* volumes. Complete copies of dissertations may be obtained from University Microfilms, Ann Arbor, Michigan.

COMPUSTAT (Standard & Poor's Corporation)

A listing of financial performance data regarding over 6000 publicly held corporations during the past 20 years.

CONGRESSIONAL INFORMATION SERVICE
1970-present, updated monthly

Guide to publications of the U.S. Congress, covering hearings, reports, committee prints, documents, and special publications of congressional committee and subcommittees.

DEADLINE DATA AND WORLD AFFAIRS
Updated weekly

Provides statistics on socioeconomic characteristics of every country in the world, each of the fifty United States, the provinces of Canada, and major international organizations.

DISCLOSURE II
Updated weekly

Indexes reports filed with the Securities and Exchange Commission by some 8800 publicly owned companies. May be accessed by company name, location, officers, SIC codes, subsidiaries, assets, revenues, or the like.

DOW JONES NEWS/RETRIEVAL
Updated continuously

News from the last 90 days that was reported in the *Dow Jones New Wire*, *Wall Street Journal*, and *Barron's*.

(continued)

TABLE 6.1 Continued

DRUG INFO
1968-present, updated quarterly

Provides coverage of the educational, psychological, medical, and sociological literature on drug and alcohol use and abuse.

ECONOMIC ABSTRACTS INTERNATIONAL
1974-present, updated monthly

Covers international literature on markets, industries, and economic reports by country.

EIST: KEY TO ENVIRONMENTAL IMPACT STATEMENTS
1977-present

Guide to environmental impact reports available through federal, state, county, and municipal agencies.

ENERGYLINE
1971-present, updated monthly

References books, articles, reports, and surveys related to energy production and consumption.

ENVIROLINE
1971-present, updated monthly

List citations related to air and water pollution, land use, environmental design, and transportation from over 5000 sources worldwide.

ERIC (Educational Resources Information Center)
1966-present, updated monthly

Indexes over 700 periodicals and hundreds of thousands of research reports, projects, and monographs in education.

EXCEPTIONAL CHILD EDUCATION RESOURCE (ECER)
1966-present, updated monthly

Includes published and unpublished literature on the education of handicapped and gifted children.

FEDERAL INDEX
1976-present, updated monthly

Guide to new federal regulations, bill introductions, speeches, hearings, executive orders, and contract awards. Indexes the *Washington Post*, *Congressional Record*, presidential documents, and *Commerce Business Daily*.

FOUNDATION DIRECTORY
annual

Describes some 3,500 foundations with assets of over $1 million or with annual grant expenditures of $100,000 or more.

(continued)

TABLE 6.1 Continued

FOUNDATION GRANTS INDEX
1973-present, updated bimonthly

Information on grants awarded by more than 400 American foundations.

GOVERNMENT PRINTING OFFICE MONTHLY CATALOG
1976-present, updated monthly

Indexes public documents generated by the U.S. government and printed by the Government Printing Office. This is equivalent to the GPO monthly catalog, only readable by a computer.

HARVARD BUSINESS REVIEW
1971-present, updated bimonthly

Offers the full text of *Harvard Business Review* from 1977 to present. Citations and abstracts are provided for earlier years (1971-1976).

HISTORICAL ABSTRACTS
1973-present

Indexes articles, dissertations, and books published outside the United States and Canada in the field of modern world history.

INFORM (Abstracted Business Information)
1971-present, updated monthly

Indexes articles from 550 major publications in business and related fields.

THE INFORMATION BANK
1974-present, updated monthly

Compiled by the *New York Times* and other major newspapers, this source provides abstracts of articles on current events from over 60 newspapers, magazines, and scientific and financial periodicals.

INSPEC (Physics, Electronics, Computers)
1969-present, updated monthly

Includes *Physics Abstracts*, *Electrical and Electronic Abstracts*, and *Computer and Control Abstracts*.

LANGUAGE AND LANGUAGE BEHAVIOR ABSTRACTS (LLBA)
1973-present, quarterly

Abstracts articles on this topic selected from 1000 worldwide journals.

LEXIS (Law)
updated continuously

Provides worldwide coverage of legal and accounting information, including the full texts of federal laws and the decisions of all federal courts.

(continued)

TABLE 6.1 Continued

M.L.A. BIBLIOGRAPHY (Literature and Language)
1970-present, annual

Indexes books and journals related to modern languages, literature, and linquistics.

MANAGEMENT CONTEXTS
1974-present, updated monthly

Includes articles from over 400 worldwide journals and other documents in all areas of management.

MEDLINE
1966-present, updated monthly

Compiled and maintained by the National Library of Medicine. Contains information on biomedical science research and on psychosocial research related to illness.

NATIONAL FOUNDATIONS
annual

Lists all U.S. foundations awarding grants. Contains over 2200 listings.

NATIONAL INSTITUTE OF MENTAL HEALTH (NIMH)
1969-present

References mental health literature selected from approximately 950 journals, symposia, government reports, and other sources, covering both biomedical and social science issues.

NATIONAL NEWSPAPER INDEX
1979-present, updated monthly

Indexes *Christian Science Monitor*, *New York Times*, *Wall Street Journal*, *Los Angeles Times*, and *Washington Post*.

NICSEM/NIMIS (National Information Center for Special Education Materials/National Instructional Materials Information System)

This index describes media and devices used with handicapped children; 1978 edition is most current.

NTIS (National Technical Information Service)
1964-present, updated biweekly

Government-sponsored research, development, and engineering. NTIS is the central source for research reports, analyses, and technical information from local, state, and federal agencies.

PAIS (Public Affairs Information Service)
1972-present, updated quarterly

Guide to publications regarding international relations, economics, public administration, law, education, social welfare, and social anthropology.

TABLE 6.1 Continued

PHARMACEUTICAL NEWS INDEX
1975-present, updated monthly
Covers all areas of pharmaceuticals, cosmetics, and the like.

PHILOSOPHERS INDEX
1940-present, updated quarterly
Indexes over 270 journals in philosophy and related fields.

POLLUTION ABSTRACTS
1970-present, updated bimonthly
Guide to technical literature on the environment in over 2500 domestic and foreign sources.

POPULATION BIBLIOGRAPHY
1966-present, updated monthly
Covers population studies, including abortion, demography, migration, family planning, fertility studies, policy, population education, and population research and methodology.

PsycINFO ABSTRACTS
1967-present, updated monthly
Covers international literature on selected topics in psychology and the behavioral sciences.

PTS
Guide to U.S. and international manufacturing, marketing and industrial forecasts. Includes several smaller databases.

SCISEARCH
1970-present, updated semimonthly
A multidisciplinary index which, by covering major journals, provides access to 90 percent of the world's significant scientific and technical literature. This database contains references from both *Science Citation Index* and *Current Contents.*

SOCIAL SCISEARCH
1972-present, updated monthly
Indexes 1000 social science journals and selected social science articles from over 2200 other journals.

SOCIOLOGICAL ABSTRACTS
1963-present, updated quarterly
Indexes world literature on sociology and related disciplines. Includes selected articles from over 1200 journals.

SSIE (Smithsonian Science Information Exchange)
Reports government and privately funded science and social science research projects either in progress or initiated and completed during the past two years. Provides name of project investigator, funding agency, summary, and detailed subject descriptors.

prices, applications, type of database, frequency of updating, and scope of the data coverage. Commercial vendors of online services, such as the Dialog Information Retrieval Service (DIALOG) and the New York Times Information Service (NYTIS), provide descriptions of the databases they offer. Table 6.1 describes a representative set of online databases, although the list is by no means exhaustive. There are numerous highly specialized services available. For example, *Coffeline* provides information relevant to the coffee industry.

The cost of an online computer search varies significantly. Royalties are charged for the use of certain proprietary databases and, of course, computer time and other resources are costly. Generally costs will range upward from $100 an hour for commercial customers, but may be less if the service is provided by a university library or a not-for-profit organization. Since most searches can be completed in fifteen to twenty minutes, the cost factor is not significant. Indeed, compared to a long, exhaustive manual search, the price of a computer search is a bargain. Most university libraries and many public and corporate libraries subscribe to one or more online information services. Access to these search capabilities is ordinarily obtained through a reference librarian, who in most cases will carry out the actual search.

SOURCES OF RAW DATA

It was noted earlier that certain raw data files are available to researchers. Several guides to these data sources are available. Table 6.2 briefly describes several of these. Prior to embarking on a primary research effort, it is useful to determine whether useful data are already available. Such data may have been collected for quite different purposes; however, it may be possible to use them in other ways.

Researchers in academic and certain not-for-profit organizations may find the Inter-University Consortium for Political and Social Research a particularly valuable source of data. The consortium is an organization of over 260 universities and colleges that was established to provide scholars at member universities with raw social science data. The consortium provides access to over 500 data files, including the following:

TABLE 6.2
Guides to Computer Data Files

Computer-Readable Data Bases: A Directory and Sourcebook (Williams, 1979)

Describes 528 international data bases. Probably the most comprehensive directory available, but not updated as frequently as others. Indexed by name, subject, producer, and processor.

Directory of Data Files

Describes all of the Census Bureau's holdings of data and information, and how they may be ordered. Abstracts for individual data files are provided.

Directory of Federal Agency Education Data Tapes

Describes available data on elementary through postsecondary education, including demographic, health and welfare, vital, and human resources statistics.

Catalog of Machine-Readable Records in the National Archives of the United States

Provides descriptions and information for ordering data files, most of which were compiled by federal agencies.

Standardized Micro-Data Tape Transcripts

A guide to NCHS data on a variety of health-related issues, ranging from human resources in health fields to vital events.

BLS Machine Readable Data and Tabulating Routines

Describes data and software routines prepared by the Bureau of Labor Statistics for distribution to researchers and users of research.

Directory of Online Databases

Describes some 770 domestic and foreign data bases and data files.

Directory of On-Line Information Resources

A guide to 300 domestic and international data files.

Information Industry Marketplace 1981: An International Directory of Information Products and Services

A comprehensive guide to companies and organizations providing computer products, supplies, and services. The publication lists database publishers, machine-readable databases, printed products derived from databases, and support services and suppliers.

- U.S. Census Data

- Current Population Survey

- Annual Housing Survey

- Panel Survey of Income Dynamics

- surveys and census data from over 130 countries other than the United States, including both current and historical data

- computer tapes of the country and city data book in each locality

- voting records of U.S. members of Congress and senators from 1789 to the present

- American National Election Study

- General Social Survey, 1972 to 1980

- polls by the Harris Organization, CBS/ *New York Times*, ABC/*Washington Post*

- Quality of Employment Survey

- National Longitudinal Survey of Labor Market Experience

- Retirement History Longitudinal Survey

- National Crime Surveys

- over 40 sets of data on war and foreign policy issues

- 40 data sets related to health issues

- 24 data sets on educational issues

Members of the consortium pay an annual affiliation fee and, with the exception of the 1980 U.S. Census data, all data are available to them at no extra charge. The consortium's headquarters are at the Center for Political Studies at the University of Michigan.

There are potential pitfalls associated with using data from these sources. First, data are not always transferable from one computer system to another, or, it they are, a significant amount of work may be required to convert and reformat the data. Second, not all databases are well documented. Thus it may not be clear how data were collected or coded. Or data may not be in a form that is optimal for a particular analysis. Levels of aggregation may be inappropriate, classifications may not match particular needs and available computer software may not be able to operate on the data as they are formatted. Finally, all of the comments in Chapter 2 concerning the evaluation of secondary sources apply to raw data as well. Despite these potential problems and limitations, the use of raw data from secondary sources offers tremendous opportunities. It is often significantly less costly than collecting one's own data. Also, because the developers of the data recognize that the data will be shared, there is an incentive to build in verification checks and to collect data that are useful to a wide range of potential users.

EXERCISES

Exercise 6.1: Identify the online computer search capabilities to which you have access. Then, design a search strategy for obtaining information concerning a topic of interest. List key words; use AND, OR, and NOT operators when appropriate; and determine how you might verify whether the computer search is reasonably complete.

Exercise 6.2: For the topic selected in Exercise 6.1, determine whether there exist any related raw data files.

7

Secondary Research
in Practice

This chapter provides two extended examples of the use of secondary information for specific problems. One illustrates a typical academic research situation; the second illustrates the solution to a common industry problem.

The first six chapters have dealt with secondary sources, the evaluation of information, and opportunities for obtaining data. Much of this material has, of necessity, been rather general and abstract. In this chapter two brief but concrete examples of the use of secondary sources are presented. The examples are not intended to be definitive or representative of applications of secondary sources, but they do provide a flavor of the nature of the task.

EXAMPLE 1:
COMMERCIAL PRACTICES AMONG
RURAL INHABITANTS OF CENTRAL AMERICA

An anthropologist at a large state university was interested in the trade practices of preindustrialized peoples and how these practices compared to those in industrialized societies. Of particular interest was Central America, since the anthropologist had previously done work in the area, had some familiarity with the customs of the people, and spoke the language. Since the anthropologist planned to write a grant proposal for support of travel to study rural Indian tribes in Central America, she had two information needs. First, she had to identify potential sources of research support. Second, she needed to do literature review in support of her grant proposal.

The researcher began the search for sources of research support with the *Annual Register of Grant Support* and the *Foundation Directory* (Lewis & Gersumky, 1981). Checking the subject index under "anthropology" and "Latin America," the researcher identified several potential sources of funding. Among these sources were the Wenner-Gren Foundation for Anthropological Research, Inc., the National Science Foundation, and the National Endowment for the Humanities. A brief letter of inquiry was addressed to each of these organizations, and the anthropologist turned her attention to the literature review.

The information search for the literature review began with three indexes: *Abstracts in Anthropology, Anthropological Literature,* and the *International Bibliography of Social and Cultural Anthropology.* All three publications were well known to the anthropologist. Under the names of various Indian tribes, Central America, commerce, and trade, the researcher found articles of interest. The humanities and social sciences volume of *Dissertation Abstracts International* was the next source consulted, followed by the *Humanities Index.* At this point the anthropologist had the names of several papers and authors and decided to use the *Social Sciences Citation Index* to determine whether other papers had cited the papers thus far identified.

The reference librarian suggested that the researcher examine several publications of Redgrave Publishing Company: *Anthropology in Use: A Bibliographic Chronology of the Development of Applied Anthropology; Anthropological Bibliographies: A Selected Guide;* and *Serial Publications in Anthropology, 1982.* In addition, the librarian recommended examining two volumes related to Latin American studies: *Handbook of Latin American Studies* and *Hispanic American Periodicals Index.* These latter publications proved particularly useful, yielding the names of various Indian tribes and geographic locations, along with specific references to publications. This information was now sufficient for the anthropologist to feel comfortable with a computer-assisted search. The researcher identified the following key words:

commerce

trade

economics

marketing

To assure that only works related to contemporary peoples were obtained in the search, she also used the NOT operator: NOT ancient, precolonial, colonial. Finally, to assure that only references related to Central America were obtained, she used the AND operator: AND Central America AND Quiche (a prominent Central American Indian tribe). (This command would limit responses to references to this particular tribe.) Thus the anthropologist used combinations of commands to create searches of the following form: commerce AND Central America NOT ANCIENT.

Within a week of the request, abstracts of papers identified in the search arrived and the anthropologist proceeded to develop her literature review.

EXAMPLE 2:
A HEALTH MAINTENANCE ORGANIZATION

An insurance company considering the establishment of a health maintenance organization (HMO) as an extension of its health care insurance product line sought to determine what was known about HMOs. A research analyst in the organization was asked to prepare a report for senior management. The report was due within a month of the request, so primary research was not practical. The analyst proceeded to the local university business library and consulted the reference librarian for sources of information about the health care industry in general and, more specifically, health maintenance organizations.

The first sources to which the analyst was referred were the *Business Index* and the *Business Periodicals Index*. Both sources were quite useful for identifying articles related to HMOs. For example, under "health" in the August 1981-July 1982 *Business Periodicals Index,* the analyst found a subheading "health maintenance organizations" and the following references:

Average HMO expects to generate 91,583 Rx's 22% more than in 1980. D. Kushner. tabs Am Druggist 184:13-14 + N '81

Bright, prognosis for the once-frail HMOs [employer sponsorship] Bus W p 108 + 0 27 '80; Same cond. compens R 13 no3:68-71 '81

Competition and health costs containment cautions and conjectures. L. D. Brown. bibl(p 187-9) Milbank Mem Fund Q/Health & Soc 59:145-89 Spr '81

HMO to open its doors after 6 1/2 year wait. C. G. Blitzer. Bus Insur 15:22 Je 15 '81

HMO, competition, and the politics of minimum benefits. D. W. Moran. bibl(207-8) Milbank Mem Fund Q/Health & Soc 59:190-208 Spr '81

HMO — medicine for feverish healthcare costs. S. G. House. Mgt World 10:32- 3 N '81

Healthy competition. Pers J 50:519-20 + J1 '81

Kaiser-Georgetown HMO suing J&H over coverage [duplicated other insurance.] J. Geisel. Bus Insur 15:6 N 2 '81

Number of new HMOs is decreasing: study. J. Geisel. Bus Insur 15:16 D 28 '81

Oregon HMO is liquidated. D.L. Yanish. Bus Insur 15:3 + N 2 '81

Private funds for what ails HMOs. Nations Bus 69:20 D '81

Through HMOs, employees gain new health care option. Sav & Loan N 102:110-00 Je '81

Union-related correlates of employee referrals to an occupational alcoholism project in a health maintenance organization. S. L. Putnam and R. L. Stout J. Occupa Med 24:255-33 Mr '82

Other issues of the *Business Periodicals Index* and the *Business Index* also yielded similar finds. The analyst proceeded to the publications referenced, read the papers, and prepared notes.

The next source consulted was the *F&S Index of Corporations and Industries*. Under the Directory of Industries and Products in the first section of this volume was a listing for health care. This listing included the SIC code for the health care industry (800010). The index included the following references:

Federal Medicare & Medicaid outlays to reach $6 bil in 1982; Reagan Admin sees spending lid WSJ(Spr) 1/22/82 p 2

Number of new health maintenance organizations is growing, with 20 new ones between June 1980-June 1981 Binsurance 12/28/81 p 16

Pharmaceutical prep sales to HMOs exceeds $160 mil in 1981 & is expected to rise 15% annually Surgical 12/81 p 12

HMO industry to appeal to private financial institutions for funds due to federal budget cuts Em Benefit 11/81 p 23

Health maintenance organizations cannot invoke the McCarran-Ferguson Act for antitrust immunity Drug Topics 1/4/82 p 2

Other editions of the index provided additional references, which the analyst noted, located, and abstracted. Notice that one problem with secondary sources has already emerged. Two publications, both appearing in December of 1981, provide contradictory information. One suggests that the number of HMOs is increasing, while the other suggests that the number is decreasing. Thus the analyst will eventually have to evaluate these two studies in light of the research methodologies employed and other available information.

FINDEX was the next source of information consulted. Several commercially available publications appeared promising:

Health Care in the United States—Social, Economic, Technical and Political Environment in the 1980s (available from the Battelle Institute for $7000.00): The summary of this document indicated that health care trends and forecasts relevant to HMOs were included in the report.

Health Industries Handbook (an annual publication of SRI International priced at $6000.00): Provides an assessment, market evaluation, and forecasts to 1984 of the health care system in the United States.

Emerging Medical Specialty Companies (available from Research from Wall Street for $140.00): A discussion of industry developments pertinent to rapidly growing companies in the health care field.

The 1982 *Predicasts Basebook* (Baumgartner, 1982) provided a more specific SIC code, one including a product code (80001304), and provided an estimate of enrollment growth (11.6 percent annual growth). The 1982 *U.S. Industrial Outlook* also provided a discussion of HMOs under the chapter on health and medical services. In addition to providing information on growth rates, several additional references were provided, including several government publications. Among the government publications identified were some particularly useful documents:

"Marketing and Enrollment Strategies for Prepaid Group Health Plans," published by the department of Health, Education and Welfare in 1972; and

"Marketing of Health Maintenance Organization Services," also published by the Department of Health, Education and Welfare, in 1971.

Finally, the analyst consulted *Abstracts of Health Care Management Studies* and *Abstracts of Hospital Management Studies,* identifying still more source material, including *Group and IPA HMOs,* a ten-year history of the Harvard Community Plan, on of the earliest HMOs; *Finance and Marketing in the Nation's Group HMOs,* published by the Group Health Association of America; and several papers in health administration journals.

Having exhausted sources already known to the analyst and those suggested by the reference librarian, the next stop in the search for information was *Statistics Sources* (Wasserman et al., 1982). This directory of directories suggested that health and medical associations might be identified by consulting the *Encyclopedia of Associations.* A number of additional source documents, primarily government documents, were consequently identified. Among the associations listed in the *Encyclopedia* was the National Association of Employers on Health Care Alternatives (NAEHCA), formerly the National Association of Health Maintenance Organizations. This organization is made up of corporations concerned with health care programs for employees. Among its publications is an annual National Survey of Health Maintenance Organizations. A call to the organization produced a copy of the survey and several additional helpful sources of information. The NAEHCA suggested contacting the American Hospital Association and consulting the *Insurance Periodicals Index* for additional information. From the American Hospital Association (1981), the analyst obtained the *American Hospital Association Guide to the Health Care Field. The Insurance Periodicals Index* provided numerous additional references.

A return to the *Encyclopedia of Associations* under the heading of insurance identified several potential sources of information. From the Health Insurance Association of America, the analyst was able to obtain the *Source Book of Health Insurance Data 1981-1982.* The National Underwriter Company provided the *1981 Time Saver for Health Insurance* (Gaines, 1981).

By this point in the analyst's search, there was a tremendous amount of information available for the report. The analyst had identified principle trade organizations, relevant academic and trade publications, forecasts for the industry, primary competitors in the field, and government regulations relevant to the industry. Still not fully satisfied, the analyst contacted the reference librarian again and requested a computer-assisted search of *Health Planning and Administration,* the database maintained by the National Library of Medicine. This computer search retrieved over 200 references to HMOs for which the analyst had abstracts printed. These were on the analyst's desk within a week. The total time required to do the information search was less than two working days. The information identified in the search was in the hands of the analyst within two weeks of the requests. The next two weeks were spent developing a summary of the literature for management. The report was well received. The analyst was named assistant to the products planning director, and was recognized as the corporate expert on HMOs.

8

Using and Integrating Secondary Information

Even when information on a topic is readily available, it is often necessary to integrate data from numerous sources in order to answer specific questions. This chapter discusses conceptual and statistical issues related to the integration and synthesis of information.

Identifying information relevant to a particular topic is only the first step in using secondary sources. It is easy to become overwhelmed by information. Finding order in a plethora of information is often difficult, particularly when there are inconsistencies, omissions, and differences in method among various sources. A common problem faced by researchers using secondary data is that of combining the findings and conclusions of several sources of information. The synthesis of information from multiple sources is an important skill, a skill that, until quite recently, suffered the criticism that it lacked objectivity (Glass, 1976). Furthermore, many users of secondary sources often come away from their efforts frustrated because they could not answer a specific question; the information dealt with issues related to the one of interest but never answered the specific question. In this chapter, information integration will be the focus. Two specific issues will be addressed: (1) how to use existing information to answer questions for which no directly accessible answer exists, and (2) how to incorporate secondary information into a more general research framework.

GENERATING ANSWERS FROM SECONDARY DATA

Answers to specific questions are frequently unavailable in secondary sources, although it is often possible to piece together such answers. For many questions and decisions, a "ball-park" figure is all that is necessary, and the creative use of existing information can often provide such estimates. Consider one of the most common questions facing organizations, the market potential question: Are there enough people (organizations) interested in our product (service) to justify our providing it? Businesses

111

ask this question about new products, universities ask this question about new programs, and government administrators often ask this question about new services. Frequently this question can be phrased as follows: Is the demand at least of size X? Consider the following illustration. In the mid-1970s, a major corporation was interested in the demand for a pet food that included both moist chunks and hard, dry chunks. The question was, "Is there currently a significant number of persons who mix moist moist or canned dog food with dry dog food?" At this early stage in the exploration of this product concept, the firm did not want to expend funds for primary research. While an actual survey of pet owners would have yielded the best answer, such a survey would have required the expenditure of several thousands of dollars. In addition, further development of the idea would have required a delay of several weeks to obtain the survey results. An effort to develop an acceptable first answer to the question of demand using secondary sources was initiated.

The firm identified the following information:

(1) From published literature on veterinary medicine, the firm identified the amount (in ounces) of food required to feed a dog each day by type of food (dry, semimoist, moist), age, size, and type of dog.

(2) From an existing survey conducted annually by the firm's advertising agency, the firm obtained information on

(a) the percentage of U.S. households owning dogs;

(b) the number, sizes, and types of dogs owned by each household in the survey;

(c) the type(s) of dog food fed to the dogs; and

(d) the frequency of use of various types of dog food.

It was assumed that dog owners who reported feeding their dogs two or more different types of dog food each day were good prospects for a product that provided premixed moist and dry food. Combining the information in the survey with the information from the literature on veterinary medicine and doing some simple multiplication produced a demand figure for the product concept. The demand exceeded 20 percent of the total volume of dog food sales, a figure sufficiently large to justify proceeding with product development and testing.

As in the above example, it is often necessary to make some assumptions in order to use secondary data. Such assumptions are often reasonable, and by altering the underlying assumptions it is frequently possible to determine how sensitive a particular conclusion is to variations in them. Such sensitivity analysis can be very useful in that it may demonstrate the need for better information or increase confidence in the initial conclusion. For example, in the illustration above, altering the assumption regarding the number of owners who were good prospects for the new product to include as few as one-tenth of the original number did not alter the decision to proceed with the product. Under such circumstances, the value of additional information would be quite small.

USING EXISTING INFORMATION
FOR PLANNING PRIMARY RESEARCH

In many cases, it is necessary to carry out new, primary research, since existing information is inadequate for the purpose at hand. Under such circumstances, secondary information may still be quite useful. Secondary sources may be useful for generating testable hypotheses, estimating base rates, developing a priori probability statements, and designing measurement instruments and sampling plans.

It is often possible to build on previous work when designing primary research. For example, prior work often provides examples of measurement instruments. These instruments, with modification where appropriate, may be incorporated into a new research project. It is not uncommon for questionnaire and test items to be borrowed from existing literature. This not only reduces the work required to develop a new research instrument, but also allows for greater comparability between previous research and the new study. Specific test items and questions are in the public domain and cannot be copyrighted, although entire questionnaires and tests may be. It is customary to cite the source of borrowed items, even when the items are not protected by law. When entire instruments are used, permission frequently must be obtained from the author(s).

Prior research may also be useful for obtaining maximal efficiencies in sample designs. The sample size (number of observations) needed for a given level of precision is a function of the variation within the population. Thus information from secondary sources may be used to ensure the desired level of precision. Furthermore, such information is necessary in order to determine the best allocation of a sampling budget. Neyman (1934) provides a useful discussion of the use of prior information for allocating research budgets. The following simple illustration provides insight into the use of secondary sources for designing a sampling plan.

Consider the case of a population that is composed of several subgroups, each of which differs in variability along some dimension. One may wish to overrepresent the groups with greater variability while under-representing groups with lesser variation. Such a procedure is known as "stratified sampling." For example, one might expect greater variations in the nature of discretionary spending in upper-income households than in lower-income households, since there is greater discretionary income available to the higher-income group. Thus oversampling of the high-income groups may be justified. Parameter estimates for the total population may be computed by correcting for the disproportionate sample sizes.

A related application of secondary sources is that of obtaining prior probability estimates for a particular event. Existing information may often be employed in conjunction with Bayes's theorem (a statistical theory) to reduce sample sizes required in further research. Since in many decision stituations a high degree of precision is not required, a very small sample size (sometimes as few as 25) may be feasible if a priori estimates can be obtained. For example, an organization considering the introduction of a new service may be interested in the reactions of potential users of the service. By obtaining information on services with similar characteristics and benefits, it may be possible to obtain an estimate of the probability distribution of relative success of these services. Given this a priori distribution (previously obtained information), a small sample of potential users may be used to compute a revised probability of success that combines the prior information with the new information. A more complete discussion of the use of this methodology may be found in Wasson (1969).

Another use of existing information is the estimation of base rates. It is often useful to know something about the frequency of events or the probability that a particular characteristic will appear in a sample of size N. Base-rate information is particularly useful in designing studies of very specific populations. For example, knowing that the incidence of a medical disorder is only 1 in 100,000 suggests that such cases may be very difficult and expensive to identify with a simple random sampling plan. Such base-rate information is also important for ensuring that diagnostic and screening procedures do not detect large numbers of false positives (Overall & Klett, 1972).

Finally, prior research is useful for identifying testable hypotheses and new avenues of research. Research funds are spent most efficiently when new knowledge is thereby gained. An examination of secondary sources provides insight into what is and is not known, the limitations of previous research, the shortcomings of methodologies employed, and the generalizability of earlier conclusions. A thorough understanding of secondary source material is the basis for developing new primary research.

INTEGRATING SECONDARY SOURCE DATA

There is a long history of attempts to integrate existing information. Literature reviews, which exist in every academic discipline and are routinely compiled by organizations, represent such efforts at integration. The potential subjectivity of such integrative efforts was mentioned above. In addition, these efforts may also be biased by a failure to incorporate all of the information available or by an imprecise weighting of the conclusions from various sources (Cooper & Rosenthal, 1980). Recently, a number of authors have suggested that statistical procedures be used to integrate existing literature (Rosenthal, 1978, 1979; Glass, 1976, 1977; Cooper, 1979; Cohen, 1977). These procedures have been referred to as "meta-analyses" (Glass, 1976, 1977). Two volumes in this series discuss in detail how such integrative analyses are conducted (Cooper, 1984; Rosenthal, 1984).

There are three basic approaches to integrating the findings of various sources. These approaches are by no means mutually exclusive; rather, they complement one another. The first, and most obvious, approach is to calculate simple summary statistics across a series of studies. The second approach involves integrating conclusions concerning experimental and treatment effects obtained in independent studies. The third approach seeks to use differences in the way information was obtained, sampling differences, differences in how measures were operationalized, and so on to determine whether such differences had a significant impact on results obtained. These three approaches are described in greater detail in the following paragraphs.

The first approach, computing simple descriptive statistics, is useful for summarizing the findings of multiple studies. Means, variances, measures of association such as Pearson product-moment correlations, and other descriptive statistics may be combined. One method for accomplishing this type of integration is a simple weighted average. For example, assume four studies from various sources report the following mean daily television viewing by persons in the United States:

	Study 1	Study 2	Study 3	Study 4
Mean (X)	5.3 hours	6.2 hours	4.8 hours	6.9 hours
Sample size (N)	200	400	100	300

A simple average of the four means would yield a result of 5.8. But this figure would be somewhat misleading because each mean is based on a different number of observations. Thus to integrate the results one should weight each individual mean by the number of observations upon which it is based, as follows:

$$\frac{(5.3)(200) + (6.2)(400) + 4.8(100) + 6.9(300)}{200 + 400 + 100 + 300} = \frac{6090}{1000} = 6.09 \text{ hours}$$

It is very important that one weight the results of studies by the number of observations, to avoid being misled. In the above example, the results were not radically different, but consider a more extreme example:

	Study 1	Study 2
Mean (X)	10	25
Sample size (N)	5	300

A simple average would yield an integrated mean of 12.5. The weighted mean would be 24.75. The weighting procedure is a simple device for placing greater emphasis on studies employing larger numbers of observations. Such weighting should also be carried out for proportions and measures of variability and association. Obviously, this weighting procedure does not account for differences other than in the number of observations. Other things being equal, however, weighting should be carried out routinely when integrating the results of multiple studies.

An even better approach to integrating descriptive statistics from multiple sources is the use of confidence intervals. Rather than arriving at a single summary statistic, the average of averages and information about means, sample size, and variability may be incorporated within a confidence interval. For example, instead of simply stating the weighted average of several results, a statement to the effect that the true mean lies between two values with a 95 percent probability may be made. For instance, the percentage of children with learning disabilities in a particular school district might be determined by studying a random sample of schoolchildren. Each child in the sample might be tested and the percentage of these children with learning disabilities used as an estimate of the incidence of learning disabilities in the total population of children. Suppose such a study was carried out, and the proportion of children with learning disabilities was found to be 15 percent. How much confidence might one place in this figure as an estimate of the percentage of children with these disabilities in the entire school district? One way to gauge confidence in this estimate is compute a confidence interval. This would take the following form: the probability is 95/100 that the actual percentage of children with learning disabilities in the entire school district is between 13 percent and 17 percent.

The use of confidence intervals provides the user with a better "feel" for the data and helps develop an appreciation for the fact that most numbers, no matter how sophisticated the procedures used to generate them, are only best guesses. The size of a confidence interval is influenced by many factors, including the size the sample and the variability of the population. Most elementary statistics texts carry a discussion of confidence intervals.

The second basic approach to integrating the findings of various sources, which is to integrate the results of experimental studies, is more complex. Rather than simply developing summary statistics describing characteristics of multiple samples, the issue is one of how much support exists for the effect of a particular treatment condition on some outcome. Suppose a school district is interested in the influence of a prekindergarten readiness program for disadvantaged children. Over the years, it may have conducted a number of studies that examined the effects of this program. In order to integrate the results of these studies, two questions must be raised. First, is there support for the hypothesis that the program affects future performance in the classroom? Second, if such influence is present, how strong is it? The first question is concerned with how to combine probability values associated with statistical tests. The second question involves estimating the variability accounted for by the effects.

When independent studies report tests of statistical significance, the probability values are important sources of information; they suggest the probability that some event could have occurred by chance alone. Statistical theory indicates that the probability of obtaining two independent events with probabilities P and Q is equal to the product (PQ). Thus, if each of two studies reject a null hypothesis at the .05 level (that is, find that real differences exist between two or more groups), the probability of obtaining two such events is $(.05)(.05) = .0025$, a rather rare event.

Consider the example of the prekindergarten readiness program above. Suppose five studies have been carried out. Three found statistical support for the effect of the program (two studies at the .05 level, one at the .10 level) and two did not (both obtained probability values of .30), although the results were in the right direction. The probability of obtaining this combination of results by chance would equal $(.10)(.05)(.05)(.30)(.30) = .0000225$, a very rare event. In many situations, this simple product is not particularly helpful since some studies may find support, others no support, and still others contradictory results. In such cases, more complex procedures are useful.

Edgington (1972a) has suggested a method for adding probabilities when the number of studies is small and the sum of the probabilities is less than one. Winer (1971) and Mosteller and Bush (1954) have also suggested more sophisticated statistical methods for combining the results for several studies. These procedures have much to recommend them, but they become cumbersome with very large numbers of studies. In such cases, a simple counting method may be useful, although this method lacks the power of other methods. With the counting method, the number of studies finding a significant experimental effect is compared with the number that would be expected by chance alone.

A number of other procedures are also available for combining the results of independent studies. These have been reviewed and compared in papers by Rosenthal (1978) and Birnbaum (1954), and in this series by Cooper (1984) and Rosenthal (1984). No one procedure appears to be best in all circumstances. Furthermore, even when such procedures suggest that particular effects may be attributable to some treatment condition(s), it is often of interest to determine the strength of the effect. Statistical significance alone does not suggest the practical importance of an effect.

There are two ways to present information on the size of an effect: One provides an estimate in terms of a correlation coefficient (the amount of variance associated with the effect); the other describes the effect in terms of a standard deviation unit (the size of the difference between outcomes when the treatment is applied versus when it is not applied). Integrating results of studies with regard to size of effect requires that information on effect size be present in each study. When this information is available, weighted averages of measures of association or difference measures provide a means for describing the strength of effects. Further discussion of such procedures may be found in Glass (1976, 1977), Cohen (1969), and Glass, McGaw, and Smith (1981).

The third and final approach to integrating research findings involves interpreting differences in the ways various studies were conducted. Differences among studies are a major source of confusion when attempting to integrate findings. Variability in measures used, sampling frames, treatment effects, and even time of data collection serve to confound the interpretation of findings and the integration of results. It is possible, and even desirable, to examine the effects of both differences and agreements across studies.

One procedure for such analyses has been suggested by Snedecor and Cochran (1967; see also Cochran & Cox, 1957; Rosenthal 1978). This procedure establishes each study (or study characteristic) as a treatment condition within an analysis of variance design. Means, sample sizes, and mean squares within treatment conditions are then compared. Use of this procedure requires substantial information about the original research and a relatively large number of studies. This approach measures the treatment × studies interaction. Significant treatment × studies interactions suggest that the source of data makes a difference in the conclusions drawn. Further examination of such interactions may suggest that one class of studies (say, those that are well designed or those using a particular subject population) tend to produce certain results, whereas other studies do not.

An interesting example of this type of analysis may be found in Farley, Lehmann, and Ryan (1981). These researchers looked at studies of the Fishbein Behavioral Intention Model (Fishbein & Ajzen, 1975) in an effort to determine whether variations in research method, type of sample, discipline in conducting the research, and several additional parameters affected the findings reported by various studies. The results of their analysis provided rather strong support for the model under investigation and suggested that sampling and research method differences did not seem to have much impact on results. For example, it did not appear that the results of tests using students as research subjects differed markedly from results using other samples. However, it also was found that results obtained by social psychologists generally provided stronger support for the model than research by investigators in marketing. This finding was particularly interesting given the differences in stimuli used and in method of presentation by researchers in these two disciplines, and suggested several new research hypotheses.

These analyses, called "generalizing from imperfect replication" by Farley et al. (1981), are very useful for integrating and synthesizing information. In addition, such analyses often suggest new research hypotheses and gaps in the existing literatures. For another example of such an analysis, see Farley, Lehmann, and Ryan (1982). Glass et al. (1981) discuss other procedures for completing such meta-analyses and provide further illustrations of the technique.

SUMMARY

Information is useful only when it is applied to a particular problem or context and integrated into a meaningful pattern. The ability to synthesize is therefore an important skill. To do so requires the availability of information about the methodologies employed in the original studies and an understanding of the tools that aid such integration. Perfect information is seldom available. Thus the evaluation of information and the integration of findings across multiple sources become critical functions, functions that require research expertise as well as knowledge of information sources.

EXERCISES

Exercise 8.1: Five studies of the relationship between scores on a college admissions test and four-year grade point averages (GPA) produced the following results:

	Study 1	Study 2	Study 3	Study 4	Study 5
Correlation between test score and GPA	.42	.38	.91	.46	.39
N	450	100	10	1500	1100

What would you conclude about the relationship between test scores and GPAs? What summary statistic would you employ to describe the results of these five studies? How do you explain the difference between the results of Study 3 and the other studies?

Exercise 8.2: Identify some areas of research where meta-analysis would be appropriate. What conditions must be met in order to perform a meta-analysis?

Exercise 8.3: For one of the areas identified in Exercise 8.2, attempt to complete a meta-analysis. What problems do you encounter? What conclusions can you draw?

REFERENCES

NOTE: Bracketed dates at the end of some entries are beginning publication dates.

Abstracts in Anthropology. (quarterly). Farmingdale, NY: Baywood [1970].
Abstracts of Health Care Management Studies. (annual). Ann Arbor: Health Administration Press for the Cooperative Information Center for Health Care Management Studies of the University of Michigan.
Abstracts of Hospital Management Studies. (quarterly). Ann Arbor: Cooperative Information Center for Hospital Management Studies, School of Public Health, University of Michigan.
Agricultural Statistics. (annual). Washington, DC: Department of Agriculture [1936].
Akey, D., Gruber, K., & Leon, L. (Eds.). (1983). *Encyclopedia of Associations* (17th ed.). Detroit: Gale Research Co.
America: History and Life. Part A: Article Abstracts and Citation. (triannual). Santa Barbara, CA: American Bibliographical Center-Clio Press.
America: History and Life. Part B: Index to Book Reviews. (biannual). Santa Barbara, CA: American Bibliographical Center-Clio Press.
American Hospital Association. (1981). *American Hospital Association guide to the health care field.* Chicago: Author.
American Statistics Index: A Comprehensive Guide and Index to the Statistical Publications of the U.S. Government (annual; monthly and quarterly updates). Washington, DC: Congressional Information Service [1973].
Annual Register of Grant Support. (annual). Chicago: Marquis Who's Who, Inc.
Annual Survey of Manufacturers. (annual). Washington, DC: Bureau of the Census.
Anthropological Literature: An Index to Periodical Articles and Essays. (quarterly). Pleasantville, NY: Redgrave [1979].
Applied Science and Technology Index. (monthly). New York: H. W. Wilson.
AUBER Bibliography. (annual). Morgantown: Bureau of Business Research, College of Business and Economics, West Virginia University for the Association for University Business and Economics Research.
Bauer, D. (1970, June). The dimensions of consumer markets abroad. *Conference Board Record.*
Baumgartner, R. (Ed.). (1982). *Predicasts basebook.* Cleveland: Predicasts, Inc.
Best's Insurance Reports (77th ed.). (1977). Oldwick, NJ: A. M. Best Co.
Bibliographic Guide to Business and Economics. (annual) Boston: G. K. Hall & Co.
BI-DATA: Printout summary. (1980). New York: Business International Corp.
Birnbaum, A. (1954). Combining independent tests of significance. *Journal of the American Statistical Association, 49,* 559-574.

BLS Handbook of Methods. (annual). Washington, DC: Bureau of Labor Statistics.

BLS machine readable data and tabulating routines. (1981). Washington, DC: Bureau of Labor Statistics.

Books in Print. (annual; monthly). New York: R. R. Bowker [1900].

Bourgue, P. J. (1974). Forecasting with Input-Output. In R. Ferber (Ed.), *Handbook of marketing research.* New York: McGraw-Hill.

Bradford's Directory of Marketing Research Agencies and Management Consultants in the U.S. and the World. (biennial). Fairfax, VA: Bradford.

British Overseas Trade Board. (1979). *International directory of published market research* (3rd ed.). London: Arlington Management Publications.

Brownstone, D. M., & Carruth, G. (1979). *Where to find business information: A worldwide guide for everyone who needs the answers to business questions.* New York: John Wiley.

Business Conditions Digest. (monthly). Washington, DC: Bureau of Economic Analysis [1961].

Business Index. (monthly). Menlo Park, Calif.: Information Access Corporation [1979].

Business information sources. (1976). Berkeley: University of California Press.

Business International. (weekly). New York: Business International Corporation.

Business Periodicals Index. (monthly). New York: H. W. Wilson [1959].

Business Statistics. (biennial). Washington, DC: Department of Commerce.

Catalog of Federal Domestic Assistance. (annual). Washington, DC: Office of Management and Budget.

Catalog of machine-readable records in the National Archives of the United States. (1977). Washington, DC: National ARchives and Records Service.

Catalog of United States Census publications, 1790-1945. (1968). Westport, CT: Greenwood.

Catalog of U.S. Census Publications. (quarterly). Washington, DC: Bureau of the Census.

Census of Agriculture. (1979). Washington, DC: Bureau of the Census.

Census of Business. (1977). Washington, DC: Bureau of the Census.

Census of Construction Industries. (1977). Washington, DC: Bureau of the Census.

Census of Governments. (1977). Washington, DC: Bureau of the Census.

Census of Housing. (1980). Washington, DC: Bureau of the Census.

Census of Manufacturers. (1977). Washington, DC: Bureau of the Census.

Census of Mineral Industries. (1977). Washington, DC: Bureau of the Census.

Census of Population. (1980). Washington, DC: Bureau of the Census.

Census of Retail Trade. (1977). Washington, DC: Bureau of the Census.

Census of Selected Service Industries. (1977). Washington, DC: Bureau of the Census.

Census of Transportation. (1977). Washington, DC: Bureau of the Census.

Census of Wholesale Trade. (1977). Washington, DC: Bureau of the Census.

A citizen's guide on how to use the Freedom of Information Act and the Privacy Act in requesting government documents. (1971). Washington, DC: Government Printing Office.

Cochran, W. G., & Cox, G. M. (1957). *Experimental designs* (2nd ed.). New York: John Wiley.

Cohen, J. (1969). *Statistical power analysis for the behavioral sciences.* New York: Academic.

Cohen, J. (1977). *Statistical power analysis for the behavioral sciences* (rev. ed.). New York: Academic.

Colgate, C., Jr., & Fowler, R. L. (Eds.). (1983). *National trade and professional associations of the United States* (18th ed.). Washington, DC: Columbia Books.

Commerce Business Daily. (daily). Chicago: Administrative Services Office, Department of Commerce.

Communication Abstracts. (quarterly). Beverly Hills, CA: Sage.

Compendium of Social Statistics. (irregular). New York: United Nations [1963].

Construction Review. (monthly). Washington, DC: Bureau of Industrial Economics.

Consultants and Consulting Organizations Directory. (biennial). Detroit: Gale Research Co.

Cooper, H. M. (1979). Statistically combing independent studies: A meta-analysis of set differences in conformity research. *Journal of Personality and Social Research, 37,* 131-146.

Cooper, H. M. (1984). *The integrative research review: A systematic approach.* Beverly Hills, CA: Sage.

Cooper, H. M., & Rosenthal, R. (1980). Statistical procedures for summarizing research findings. *Psychological Bulletin, 87,* 442-449.

Corporate Profiles for Executives and Investors. (annual). Chicago: Rand McNally.

Corporation Records. (quarterly). New York: Standard & Poor's Corporation.

County and City Data Book: A Statistical Abstract Supplement (Regions, Divisions, States, Counties, Metropolitan Areas, Cities). (biannual). Washington, DC: Bureau of the Census.

County Business Patterns. (annual). Washington, DC: Bureau of the Census [1943].

Crop Production. (annual). Washington, DC: Department of Agiculture.

Crop Values. (annual). Washington, DC: Department of Agriculture.

Cultural directory: Guide to federal funds and services for cultural activities. (1975). New York: Associated Council for the Arts.

Current Construction Reports. (monthly). Washington, DC: Bureau of Industrial Economics.

Current Housing Reports. (annual). Washington, DC: Bureau of the Census.

Current Index to Journals in Education. (annual). Washington, DC: National Institute of Education.

Current Industrial Reports. (monthly). Washington, DC: Bureau of the Census.

Current Population Reports. (annual). Washington, DC: Bureau of the Census.

Datapro directory of online services. (1983). Delron, NJ: Datapro Research Corporation.

Defense Indicators. (monthly). Washington, DC: Bureau of Economic Analysis [1969].

Demographic Yearbook. (annual). New York: United Nations [1948].

Digest of Educational Statistics. (annual). Washington, DC National Center for Education Statistics [1962].

Directory Information Service Guide. (triannual). Detroit: Information Enterprises.

Directory of American Firms Operating in Foreign Countries. (annual). New York: World Trade Academic Press.

Directory of data files. (1979). Washington, DC: Bureau of the Census.

Directory of data sources on racial and ethnic minorities. (1975). Washington, DC: Bureau of Labor Statistics.

Directory of directories. (1983). Detroit: Gale Reseach Co.

Directory of European associations. (1976) Detroit: Gale Research Co.

Directory of federal agency education data tapes. (1976). Washington, DC: National Center for Education Statistics.

Directory of federal statistical data files. (1981) Washington, DC: National Technical Information Service and Office of Federal Statistical Policy and Standards.

Directory of industry data sources: The United States of America and Canada. (1981). Cambridge, MA: Ballinger.

Directory of international statistics. (1975). New York: United Nations.

Directory of occupational titles. (1962; 1975 update). Washington, DC: Department of Labor.

Directory of Online Databases. (quarterly). Santa Monica, CA: Cuadra Associates [1980].

Directory of On-Line Information Resources. (biennial). Kensington, MD: CSG Press [1978].

Directory of United Nations information systems and services (2nd ed.). (1978) New York: United Nations.

Dissertation Abstracts International: Abstracts of Dissertations Available on Microfilm or as Xerographic Reproductions. (annual/monthly). Ann Arbor, MI: University Microfilms International [1938].

Doing business in Canada. (1979). New York: Price Waterhouse.

Dow Jones averages 1885-1970. (1972). Princeton, NJ: Dow Jones Books.

Dow Jones Investor's Handbook. (annual). New York: Dow Jones and Co.

Dun & Bradstreet Million Dollar Directory. (annual) New York: Dun & Bradstreet, Inc.

Dun & Bradstreet Principal International Businesses. (annual). New York: Dun & Bradstreet, Inc.

Dun's business rankings. (1982). New York: Dun & Bradstreet, Inc.

Dun's Financial Profiles. (custom). New York: Dun and Bradstreet, Inc.

Economic Indicators. (monthly). Washington, DC: Council of Economic Advisers.

Economic Report of the President. (annual). Washington, DC: Office of the President of the United States.

Edgington, E. S. (1972a). An additive method for combining probability values from independent experiments. *Journal of Psychology, 80,* 351-363.

Edgington, E. S. (1972b). A normal curve method for combining probability values from independent experiments. *Journal of Psychology, 82,* 85-89.

EIA Data Index: An Abstract Journal. (biannual). Washington, DC: Energy Information Administration [1980].

EIA Publications Directory: A User's Guide. (biannual). Washington, DC: Energy Information Administration [1980] (semiannual).

EIS Establishments. (custom). New York: Economic Information Systems, Inc.

EIS Plants. (custom). New York: Economic Information Systems, Inc.

Emerging medical specialty companies. (1979). New York: Research from Wall Street.

Employment and Earnings. (monthly). Washington, DC: Bureau of Labor Statistics.

Employment and Earnings Statistics for States and Areas. (annual). Washington, DC: Bureau of Labor Statistics [1939].

Employment and Earnings Statistics for the United States. (annual). Washington, DC: Bureau of Labor Statistics [1909].

Encyclopedia of Associations. (every other year). Detroit: Gale Research Co. [1982].

Engineering Index. (monthly). New York: Engineering Index Incorporated.

Eskin, G. (1981, September 18). Advances in scanner based research systems yield fast, accurate new product test results. *Marketing News,* p. 20.

Ethnic statistics: A compendium of references sources. (1978). Arlington, VA: Data Use and Access Laboratories.

Ethnic statistics: Using national data resources for ethnic studies. (1978). Arlington, VA: Data Use and Access Laboratories.

F&S Index to Corporations and Industries. (annual, quarterly, monthly, weekly). Cleveland: Predicasts, Inc. [1960].

Factfinder for the Nation. (irregular). Washington, DC: Bureau of the Census [1976].

Farley, J. U., Lehmann, D. R., & Ryan, M. J. (1981). Generalizing from imperfect replication. *Journal of Business, 54,* 597-610.

Farley, J. U., Lehmann, D. R., & Ryan, M. J. (1982). Patterns in parameters of buyer behavior models: Generalizing from sparse replication. *Marketing Science, 1,* 181-204.

Farrell, M. L. (Ed.). (annual). *Barron's Market Laboratory.* Princeton, NJ: Dow Jones Books.

Federal Budget in Brief. (annual). Washington, DC: Office of Management and Budget [1951].

Federal Evaluations. (irregular). Washington, DC: General Accounting Office. (Last published 1980.)

Federal Register. (daily). Washington, DC: Office of the Federal Register.

Federal Register Index. (monthly). Washington, DC: Government Printing Office.

Federal Reserve Bulletin. (monthly). Washington, DC: Board of Governors of the Federal Reserve System [1915].

Federal Reserve Chart Book. (quarterly). Washington, DC: Board of Governors of the Federal Reserve System [1947].

Federal Reserve Historical Chart Book. (annual). Washington, DC: Board of Governors of the Federal Reserve System [1947].

Federal Statistical Directory. (annual). Washington, DC: Office of Management and Budget [1951].

FINDEX: The directory of market research reports, studies and surveys. (1982). New York: FIND/SVP.

Fishbein, M., & Ajzen, I. (1975). *Belief, attitude, intention and behavior: An introduction to theory and research.* Reading, MA: Addison-Wesley.

Fiske, D. W. (1971). *Measuring the concepts of personality.* Chicago: Aldine.

Foreign Agricultural Trade of the United States. (monthly). Washington, DC: Department of Agriculture, Economics, Statistics, and Cooperatives Service, [1962].

Fortune Double 500 Directory, Fortune Magazine (May-August). (annual). New York: Time, Inc.

Fowler, F. J., Jr. (1984). *Survey research methods.* Beverly Hills, CA: Sage.

Gaines, P. (Ed). (1981). *1981 time saver for health insurance.* Cincinnati: National Underwriter Co.

Glass, G. V (1977). Integrating findings: The meta-analysis of research. *Review of Research in Education, 5,* 351-379.

Glass, G. V (1976). *Primary, secondary, and meta-analysis of research.* Paper presented at the meeting of the American Educational Research Association, San Francisco.

Glass, G. V , McGaw, B., & Smith, M. L. (1981). *Meta-analysis in social research.* Beverly Hills, CA: Sage.

Guide to American directories (10th ed.). (1978). Coral Springs, FL: B. Klein.

Guide to American scientific and technical directories (2nd ed.). (1975). Coral Springs, FL: B. Klein.

Guide to federal statistics, a selected list. (1980). Washington, DC: Department of Commerce.

Guide to Grant and Award Programs. (annual). Bethesda, MD: National Institutes of Health.

Guide to USDA statistics. (1973). Washington, DC: Department of Agriculture.

Guide to U.S. Government Statistics (7th ed.). (1978-1979; quarterly supplements). McLean, VA: Documents Index.

Haas, R. W., (1977). SIC systems and related data for more effective market research. *Industrial Marketing Management,* 6, 429-435.

Hamilton, M. C. (1974). *Directory of educational statistics: A guide to sources.* Ann Arbor, MI: Pierian Press.

Handbook of Basic Economic Statistics. (annual; monthly supplements). Washington, DC: Economic Statistics Bureau.

Handbook of cyclical indicators (1977). Washington, DC: Bureau of Economic Analysis.

Handbook of economic statistics (1980). Washington, DC: Central Intelligence Agency.

Handbook of Labor Statistics (annual). Washington, DC: Bureau of Labor Statistics [1926].

Handbook of Latin American Studies. (annual). Austin, TX: University of Texas Press [1935].

Hauser, P. M. (1975). *Social statistics in use.* New York: Russell Sage.

Health Care in the United States: Social, economic technical, and political environment in the 1980s. (1982). Cleveland: Battelle.

Health Industries Handbook Annual. (annual). Palo Alto, CA: SRI International.

Hispanic American Periodicals Index. (annual). Los Angeles: UCLA Latin American Center Publications [1975].

Historical Abstracts. (quarterly). Santa Barbara, CA: American Biographical Center [1955].

Historial statistics of the United States: Colonial times to 1970. (1975). Washington, DC: U.S. Bureau of the Census.

Housing and Urban Development Statistical Yearbook. (annual). Washington, DC: Department of Housing and Urban Development [1969].

Human Resources Abstracts: An International Information Service. (quarterly). Beverly Hills, CA: Sage [1966].

Humanities Index. (quarterly). New York: H. W. Wilson Co. [1974].

Index Medicus. (monthly). Bethesda, MD: National Library of Medicine.

Index of international public opinion 1981-1982. (1982). Westport, CT: Greenwood.

Index to Latin American Periodical Literature. (annual). Boston: G. K. Hall [1929-1969].

Index to legal periodicals. (1979). Washington, DC: George Washington University.

Index to 1980 census summary tapes. (1982). Washington, DC: Bureau of the Census.

Index to selected 1980 census reports. (1982). Washington, DC: Bureau of the Census.

Industrial research laboratories of the United States (15th ed.). (1977). New York: Bowker.

Information industry marketplace 1981: An international directory of information products and services (2nd ed.). (1980). New York: Bowker.

Insurance Periodicals Index. (annual). New York: Insurance Division, Special Libraries Association.

International bibliography of Social and Cultural Anthropology. (annual). New York: Tavistock [1955].

International Business Year Book. (annual). London: Financial Times.

International Directory of Marketing Research Houses and Services. (annual). New York: American Marketing Association, New York Chapter.

Irregular serials and annuals: An international directory (8th ed.). (1983). New York: Bowker.

Jablonski, D. M. (Ed.). (1979). *How to find information about companies.* Washington, DC: Washington Researchers.

Katzer, J., Cook, K. H., & Crouch, W. W. (1978). *Evaluating information: A guide for users of social science research.* Reading, MA: Addison-Wesley.

Kelly's Manufacturers and Merchants Directory. (annual). Kingston Upon Thames: Kelly's Directories.

Kruazas, A. T., & Sullivan, L. V. (1978). *Encyclopedia of information systems and services* (3rd ed.). Detroit: Gale Research Co.

Lewis, M. O., & Gersumky, A. T. (Eds.). (1981). *The foundation directory* (8th ed.). New York: Foundation Center.

Local area personal income 1971-76. (1978). Washington, DC: Bureau of economic Analysis.

Long term economic growth: 1860-1970 (2nd ed.). (1973). Washington, DC: Bureau of Economic Analysis.

Major programs 1980: Bureau of Labor Statistics. (1980). Washington, DC: Bureau of Labor Statistics.

Maloney, J. F. (1976, July 2). In Saudi Arabia, sands, statistics can be shifty. *Marketing News*, p. 6.

Management Contents. (biweekly). Skokie, IL: G. D. Searle and Co. [1975].

Marketing Economics: Key Plants. (biennial). New York: Marketing Economics Institute, Ltd.

Marketing Information Guide. (monthly). Garden City, NY: Hoke Communications.

Master Key Index. (quarterly). New York: Business International Corporation.

May, E. G. (1979). *A handbook on the use of government statistics.* Charlottesville, VA: Taylor Murphy Institute.

Measuring markets: A guide to the use of federal and state statistical data. (1979). Washington, DC: Industry and Trade Administration, Department of Commerce.

Mediamark Research. (annual). New York: Mediamark Reseach, Inc.

Mental Health Abstracts. (monthly). Rockville, MD: National Clearinghouse for Mental Health Information, National Institute of Mental Health [1969].

Merchandising. (annual). New York: Billboard Publications.

Monthly Bulletin of Statistics. (monthly). New York: United Nations [1947].

Monthly Catalog of U.S. Government Publications. (monthly). Washington, DC: Government Printing Office [1895].

Monthly Labor Review. (monthly). Washington, DC: Bureau of Labor Statistics [1915].

Monthly Report on the Labor Force. (monthly). Washington, DC: Bureau of Labor Statistics.

Monthly Retail Trade. (monthly). Washington, DC: Bureau of the Census.

Monthly Selected Service Receipts. (monthly). Washington, DC: Bureau of the Census.

Monthly Vital Statistics Report. (monthly). Hyattsville, MD: Department of Health and Human Services, Public Health Service.

Monthly Wholesale Trade: Sales and Inventories. (monthly). Washington, DC: Bureau of Census.

Moody's international manual. (1982). New York: Moody's Investors Service, Inc.

Moody's Manuals. (annual; supplement). New York: Moody's Investors Service, Inc.

Mosteller F. M., & Bush, R. R. (1954). Selected quantitative techniques. In G. Lindzey (Ed.), *Handbook of social psychology: Vol. 1. Theory and method. Cambridge, MA: Addison-Wesley.*

National Technical Information Service [NTIS]. (1975). *National environmental statistical report*. Arlington, VA: Mitre Corp.

National Trade and Professional Associations of the United States and Canada and Labor Unions. (annual). Washington, DC: Columbia Book.

New York Times Index. (semimonthly). New York: New York Times [1913].

Neyman, J. (1934). On the two different aspects of the representative method: The method of stratified sampling and the method of purposive selection. *Journal of the Royal Statistical Society, 97*, 558-606.

NIH Research Contracting Process. (annual). Bethesda, MD: National Institutes of Health.

Norback, C. T. (1980). *Corporate publications in print*. New York: McGraw-Hill.

Overall, J. E., & Klett, J. C. (1972). *Applied multivariate analysis*. New York: McGraw-Hill.

Pas, H.T.V. (1973). *Economic anthropology, 1940-1972: An annotated bibliography*. Osterhout, Netherlands: Anthropological Publications.

Personnel Management Abstracts. (quarterly). Ann Arbor: Graduate School of Business Administration, University of Michigan.

Pick's Currency Yearbook. (annual). New York: Pick Publishing Corp.

Population Bibliography. (bimonthly). Chapel Hill: University of North Carolina, Carolina Population Center [1966].

Predicasts Forecasts. (annual/quarterly). Cleveland: Predicasts, Inc.

Price Waterhouse Guide Series. (annual). New York: Price Waterhouse and Co.

PRIZM adds zip to consumer research. (1980, November 10). *Advertising Age*, p. 22.

Publication Yearbook. (annual). Rome: Food and Agriculture Organization of the United Nations.

Progressive Grocer. (monthly). Stamford, CT: Maclean Hunter Media, Inc.

Projections of Educational Statistics. (annual). Washington DC: National Center for Education Statistics. [1962].

Psychological Abstracts: Nonevaluative Summaries of the World's Literature in Psychology and Related Disciplines. (monthly). Arlington, VA: American Psychological Association [1927].

Public Affairs Information Service bulletin: A Selected Subject List of the Latest Books, Pamphlets, Government Publications, Reports of Public and Private Agencies and Periodical Articles, Relating to Economic and Social Conditions, Public Administration and International Relations, Published in English throughout the World. (monthly). New York: Public Affairs Information Service. [1914].

Reader's Guide to Periodical Literature. (semimonthly). New York: H. W. Wilson Co. [1900].

Research centers directory (6th ed.). (1979). Detroit: Gale Research Co.

A Researcher's Guide to Washington. (annual). Washington, DC: Washington Researchers [1973].

Riche, M. F. (1983, February). Data companies 1983. *American Demographics*, pp. 28-39.

Rosenthal, R. (1978). Combining results of independent studies. *Psychological Bulletin, 85*, 185-193.

Rosenthal, R. (1979). The "file drawer problem" and tolerance for null results. *Psychological Bulletin, 86*, 638-641.

Rosenthal, R. (1984). *Meta-analytic procedures for social research*. Beverly Hills, CA: Sage.

Rosenthal, R., & Rubin, D. B. (1979). Comparing significance levels of independent studies. *Psychological Bulletin, 86*, 1165-1168.

Sage Public Administration Abstracts. (quarterly). Beverly Hills, CA: Sage [1974].

Sales and Marketing Management. (monthly). New York: Sales and Marketing Management [1918].

Science Citation Index. (quarterly). Philadelphia: Institute for Scientific Information [1969].

Science Indicators. (biennial). Washington, DC: National Science Board [1972].

Sheldon's Retail Directory of the United States and Canada. (annual). New York: Phelon, Sheldon, and Marsar, Inc.

Singer, M. (1971). The vitality of mythical numbers. *Public Interest, 23,* 3-9.

Smith, M. L., & Damien, Y. M. (Eds.). (1982). *Anthropological bibliographies: A selected guide.* South Salem, NY: Redgrave.

Snedecor, G. W., & Cochran, W. G. (1967). *Statistical methods* (6th ed.). Ames: Iowa State University Press.

Social indicators 1976. (1977). Washington, DC: Department of Commerce.

Social Science Index. (monthly). New York: H. W. Wilson Co. [1974].

Social Sciences Citation Index: An International Multidisciplinary Index to the Literature of the Social, Behavioral, and Related Sciences. (quarterly). Philadelphia: Institute for Scientific Information [1973].

Sociological Abstracts. (monthly). San Diego: Sociological Abstracts [1952].

Source Book for Criminal Justice Statistics. (annual). Washington, DC: National Criminal Justice Information and Statistics Service [1973].

Source book of health insurance data 1981-1982. (1981). Washington, DC: Public Relations Division, Health Insurance Association of America.

Standard & Poor's Register of Corporations, Directors, and Executives. (annual). New York: Standards & Poor's Corp.

Standard & Poor's Stock Reports. (annual). New York: Standard & Poor's Corp.

Standard Industrial classification manual. (1972; 1977 supplement). Washington, DC: Office of Management and Budget.

Standard Rate and Data Service. (monthly). Skokie, IL: Standard Rate and Data Service, Inc.

Standardized micro-data tape transcripts. (1976). Washington, DC: National Center for Health Statistics.

Stateman's Yearbook. (annual). London: Macmillan [1864].

Statistical Abstract of the United States. (annual). Washington, DC: Bureau of the Census.

Statistical Reference Index. (annual). Washington, DC: Congressional Information Service [1980].

Statistical services of the United States government (rev. ed.). (1975). Washington, DC: Office of Management and Budget, Statistical Policy Division.

Statistics of Income. (annual). Washington, DC: Internal Revenue Service [1916].

Statistics of the Communications Industry in the U.S. (annual). Washington, DC: Federal Communications Commission [1939].

A student's workbook on the 1970 census. (1976). Washington, DC: Bureau of the Census.

Survey of Current Business. (monthly). Washington, DC: Bureau of Economic Analysis [1921].

Sudman, S., & Ferber, R. (1979). *Consumer panels.* Chicago: American Marketing Association.

Tax, S., & Grollig, F. X. (1982). *Serial publications in anthropology 1982.* South Salem, NY: Redgrave.

Thomas Register of American Manufacturers. (annual). New York: Thomas.

Trade and Industry Index. (monthly). Menlo Park, CA: Information Access Corp. [1981].

Trade Directories of the World. (monthly). Queens Village, NY: Croner.

Ulrich's International Periodicals Directory. (biennial). New York: Bowker.

UNESCO Statistical Yearbook. (annual). Paris: United Nations Educational, Scientific, and Cultural Organization [1963].

Uniform Crime Reporting. (quarterly). Washington, DC: Federal Bureau of Investigation.

Uniform Crime Reports for the United States. (annual). Washington, DC: Federal Bureau of Investigation [1930].

United Nations Statistical Yearbook. (annual). New York: United Nations [1949].

United States Government Manual. (annual). Washington, DC: Office of the Federal Register, General Services Administration.

United States Political Science Documents. (annual). Pittsburgh: University of Pittsburgh [1975].

Urban Affairs Abstracts. (weekly; quarterly and annual cumulations). Washington, DC: National League of Cities [1971].

U.S. Industrial Outlook. (annual). Washington, DC: Industry and Trade Administration.

Value Line Investment Survey. (quarterly; weekly supplements). New York: A. Bernhard and Co.

Van Willigen, J. (1982). *Anthropology in use: A bibliographic chronology of the development of applied anthropology.* South Salem, NY: Redgrave.

Vital Statistics of the United States. (annual). Washington, DC: National Center for Health Statistics [1937].

Vital Statistics Report. (monthly). Washington, DC: Department of Health and Human Services.

Wall, C. E. (Ed.). (annual). *Consumers Index.* Ann Arbor, MI: Pierian Press.

Wall Street Journal Index. (monthly). Princeton, NJ: Dow Jones Books [1957].

Wasserman, P., & Morgan, J. (Eds.). (1978). *Consumer sourcebook.* Detroit: Gale Research Co.

Wasserman, P., O'Brien, J., Grace, D. A., & Clansky, K. (Eds.). (1982). *Statistics sources* (7th ed.). Detroit: Gale Research Co.

Wasserman, P., Sanders, J., & Sanders, E. T. (1978). *Encyclopedia of geographic information sources* (3rd ed.). Detroit: Gale Research Co.

Wasson, C. (1969). *Understanding quantitative analysis.* New York: Appleton-Century-Crofts.

Wasson, C. (1974). Use and appraisal of existing information. In R. Ferber (Ed.), *Handbook of marketing research.* New York: McGraw-Hill.

Wasson, C. R., & Shreve, R. R. (1976). *Interpreting and using quantitative aids to business decision.* Austin, TX: Austin.

Weckesser, T. C., Whaley, J. R., & Whaley, M. (Eds.). (1978). *Business services and information: The guide to the federal government.* New York: John Wiley.

Weise, F. (Ed.). (1980). *Health Statistics: A guide to information sources.* Detroit: Gale Research Co.

Wheeler, M. (1977). *Lies, damn lies and statistics.* New York: Dell.

Who Owns Whom. (annual). New York: Dun & Bradstreet International, Ltd.

Who's Who in America. (biennial). Chicago: Marquis Who's Who.

Williams, M. E. (1979). *Computer-readable data bases: A directory and sourcebook.* Washington, DC: American Scoiety for Information Science.

Williamson, M. J. (Ed.). (1979). *Statistical information sources: A guide for financial institutions.* Park Ridge, Ill: Bank Administration Institute.

Winer, B. J. (1971). *Statistical principles in experimental design* (2nd ed.). New York: McGraw-Hill.

Work Related Abstracts. (monthly). Detroit: Information Coordinators, Inc.

World Advertising Expenditures. (annual). New York: Starch INRA Hooper.

World Economic Survey. (annual). New York: United Nations [1947].

World Health Statistics Annual. (annual). Geneva: World Health Organization [1969].

World Statistics in Brief. (annual). New York: United Nations [1976].

Worldcasts. (quarterly). Cleveland: Predicasts, Inc.

AUTHOR INDEX

SUBJECT INDEX

Bureau of Economic Analysis (BEA), 62-63

Bureau of the Census, 29, 35-43, 100; Census of Business, 37; Census of Construction Industries, 38; Census of Governments, 38; Census of Manufacturers, 37; Census of Mineral Industries, 38; Census of Transportation, 12, 37; data tapes, 36, 39, 40; Decennial Census of Housing, 37; Decennial Census of the Population, 14, 37, 40-41, 49, 50-51; tract reports, 40-41, 47-50; guides to data, 39-40; Quinquennial Census of Agriculture, 38;

Central Intelligence Agency, 64

Computer software, 91; Bureau of the Census, 36-37; Financial Marketing Group, Inc., 75; geographic systems, 75; International Data and Development (IDD), 76; Urban Sciences Applications, Inc., 78; Vistar, Inc., 79; Wharton EFA, Inc., 79;

Computer-assisted information search, 91-93, 100, 106, 110

Congressional Information Service, 64

Corporate information, 80, 82-84

Corporate publications, 79-80

Council of Economic Advisers, 62

Court records, 65

Customized research services, 72, 79; Bureau of the Census, 39, 49; Burke Marketing Research, 8; guides to, 72, 79;

Databases, 93-100; Bureau of the Census, 36; Chase Econometrics, 73; DUALabs, 75; Donnelly Marketing,

75; Geographic Systems, 75; guides to, 101; LEXIS (law), 93, 97; National Library of Medicine, 110; Orrington Economics, Inc., 77; Sammamish Data Systems, 78; Wharton EFA, Inc., 79

Demographic data firms, 73-79; Allstate Research and Planning Center, 73; CACI, 73; Chase Econometrics, 73; Claritas, 73; Compucon, 73; Compusearch, 73; Criterion, 74; Data Resources, Inc., (DRI), 74; Datamap, 74; Demographic Research Company, 74; Distribution Sciences, 74; Donnelley Marketing, 75; DUALabs, 75; Financial Marketing Group, inc., 75; Geographic Data Technology, 75; Geographic Systems, 75; Infomap, 75; International Data and Development, (IDD), 76; Kellex, 76; Market Statistics, 76; Metromail, 76; Modeling Systems, 76; National Decision Systems, 76; National Planning Data Corporation, 77; Orrington Economics, Inc., 77; Personnel Research, Inc. (PRI), 77; Public Demographics, Inc., 77; R. L. Polk and Co., 77; Robinson Associates, 78; Sammamish Data Systems, 78; Survey Sampling, 78; Urban Data Processing, 78; Urban Decision Systems, 78; Urban Science Applications, Inc., 78; Vistar, Inc., 78; Warren Glimpse and Co., 79; Wharton EFA, Inc., 79

Department of Agriculture (DOA), 60

ABOUT THE AUTHOR

David W. Stewart is Associate Professor of Management at the Owen Graduate School of Management, Vanderbilt University. He received his Ph.D. in psychology from Baylor University and served as a research manager for a major advertising agency prior to entering the teaching profession. His publications have appeared in the *Journal of Marketing Research, Journal of Applied Psychology, Journal of the Academy of Management, Journal of Advertising, Journal of Consumer Research,* and numerous other journals and published proceedings. He is an active consultant to management, Associate Editor of *Psychology and Marketing,* and a frequent guest lecturer. His teaching interests include consumer behavior, marketing research, and decision theory.